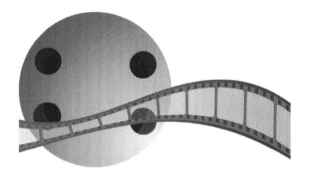

LIFE SCRIPT RESTRUCTURING

The Neuroplastic Psychology for Rewiring Your
Brain and Changing Your Life

LIFE SCRIPT RESTRUCTURING

The Neuroplastic Psychology for Rewiring Your
Brain and Changing Your Life

DR. GALEN E. COLE

Aphalon Firth, an imprint of
Aphalon Firth Publishing Company

CONTENTS

CONTENTS

PREFACE

My entire professional career has consisted of conducting research and working with populations and individuals to help them overcome problems and ultimately reach their full potential. Throughout this time my clinical tool of choice has always been Cognitive Behavioral Therapy (CBT), which is described in my book, True Psychology: A Scientific Approach to a Better Life. Frankly, for many years, CBT has been the only psychotherapy that has consistently proven effective in clinical trials.

The premise of CBT is relatively simple. It focuses on the idea that people can be taught to think and act in more rational (effective) ways. This approach not only provides a means of changing the ways people view themselves and their environment (cognitions), but also the way they act in that environment (behaviors).

In my experience, the only downside to CBT has been the prescribed focus on helping individuals identify and change one irrational thought at a time. Because it's estimated that the average person thinks between 20,000 and 70,000 thoughts per day, you can image how inefficient it can be to focus on changing a single irrational thought. With this limitation in mind, I have struggled to find a more efficient approach to helping individuals deal with a broader range of issues.

Ironically, I discovered what has proven to be a more effective path inside a Hollywood Studio. This discovery took place when I was consulting on a popular television program. I was sitting in a Hollywood studio with several writers and a producer discussing the different ways one of the characters on the program might respond to a number of "hypothetical" challenges in her life. For the first time, it occurred to me that what was happening in the studio was very much like what happens in my clinics.

As I answered questions about different scenarios, the writers were editing the story line, which would eventually be passed off to the actors in the form of a script. The actors would, in turn, rehearse their lines and play their parts.

This is also true with my clients. They listen and think through my Socratic questions and suggestions, and based on their insights they will change their "life script." In fact, I now tell all my clients that a necessary first step in improving their lives is to systematically identify and revise stories they tell themselves that undermine their success and happiness.

This new approach, which I call Life Script Restructuring (LSR), has been highly successful in helping individuals revise destructive internal narratives and thereby change their lives for good. Because of this success I have written this book to make this incredibly effective approach available to the masses.

I have discovered first-hand through my research and the work I have done among various cultures around the globe that anyone, anywhere who is willing to invest the time required to write a new Life Script and to rehearse the script using the self-hypnosis techniques I outline in my book will be able to permanently change his or her life.

Contemporary Neurological Research has demonstrated that our brains have the ability to rewire themselves in response to changes in our thinking. This characteristic of the brain is called Neuroplasticity.

LSR systematically leverages brain plasticity in a way that allows you to painlessly unlearn maladaptive ways of thinking and living and permanently replace them with rational Life Scripts that perpetually dictate rational thoughts and actions.

Although this process is similar to modern CBT, I have discovered it to be more efficient and effective. This is because instead of attempting to change how you see the world, one irrational thought at a time, through LSR you are able to contextualize and change the entire infrastructure of your many Life Scripts that, at both a subconscious and conscious level, persistently dictate everything you think and do.

As was mentioned above, this process is important because you think thousands of discrete thoughts every day. To make sense of these thoughts, you organize them into stories. The irrational stories (irrational Life Scripts) you tell yourself are the targets of LSR.

> The idea that the brain can change its own structure and function through thought and activity is, I believe, the most important alteration in our view of the brain since we first sketched out its basic anatomy and the workings of its basic component, the neuron. - Norman

Finally, let me say that this approach is not simply another self-help book that is based on what I predict might work to help others improve their lives. I cannot imagine sitting across from clients day after day trying to persuade them to do something that does not work. LSR works because it's grounded in my clinical experience and based on what leading behavioral scientists agree are the key universal principles required to help individuals make permanent changes and reach their potential.

Obviously, I recommend that you read this book and begin the process of rewriting the parts of your Life Script that are not currently working for you. After all, you are the star of the "movie about your life," and the scripts you write and play out will determine whether or not you will live the kind of life you want to live and experience a happy ending!

No man can run away from weakness. He must either fight it out or perish. And if that be so . . . why not now, and where you stand. - Robert Louis Stevenson

PROLOGUE
SETTING THE STAGE FOR LIFE
SCRIPT RESTRUCTURING

This prologue consists of an introduction and an explanation of the core principle that you will need to understand to engage in the Life Script Restructuring (LSR) process. The core principle discussed and applied across the entire LSR process is Rationality.

INTRODUCTION TO THE LSR PROCESS

After you learn the principles outlined here, the LSR process will include four ACTS. ACT I involves determining what you want to happen in your life over the short and long term. This includes looking at your vision of your future and your goals related to this vision. ACT II takes you through a process of identifying destructive internal narratives (irrational Life Scripts) that undermine your ability to achieve your goals and realize your vision. ACT III helps you restructure irrational Life Scripts into rational Life Scripts which, when followed, help you get what you want in life and live the kind of life you want to live. Finally, ACT IV explains how to mentally program your new Life Scripts so that they subtly and persistently guide both your unconscious and conscious thoughts and actions and how to protect your new scripts and the lifestyle they produce from forces that can cause you to revert back to your old ways of thinking and acting.

Everyone has a story, make yours worth telling.
- Patrick Ricketts

When I teach this approach to changing maladaptive thinking, I often use analogies from my work in Hollywood (Greenberg, et. al., 2004), where I have observed writers changing scripts based on my input about different characters. For example, on one occasion I was speaking to script writers about a character they had decided would eventually get tested for the BRCA 1/2 genes (human genes that can be tested to identify an increased risk of female breast and ovarian cancer) to determine if she was at increased risk for getting cancer. During our discussion, the writers were editing their script based on my input. These edits were incorporated into the final script, which dictated how the female character would play her part in an eight-episode story ARC (Rosenthal, de Castro-Buffington, Cole, 2013).

My experience with Hollywood writers serves as a great metaphor for Life Script Restructuring, which is designed to help you identify Life Scripts that need to be edited or changed in a way that helps you live the kind of life you want to live. Once you, the producer of your life and the main character in each of your Life Scripts, learn to write rational Life Scripts, rehearse them until they are believable, and then play the part you have outlined for your life, you will be able to consistently manufacture the kind of life you want to live. As my wife once said to me as I was explaining this analogy, "I think you are saying this means that every person is the writer and producer of their own lives, and to get different results you need to change the script—put the information together differently."

All of this is possible because the LSR process is designed to help you leverage brain plasticity in a way that allows you to systematically re-engineer or reprogram your beliefs, thoughts, actions, and how you view yourself in a way that will enlarge, deepen, broaden, and amplify your highest aspirations for happiness, health, and serenity (Deiner, 2000; Seligman, 2012). In other words, changing your Life Script can fundamentally change your core beliefs, heart, and life.

THE RATIONALITY PRINCIPLE APPLIED TO LSR

The most important principle required to understand the LSR process is the concept of rationality. This is because across the entire LSR process, you will be deciding whether or not your thoughts and Life Scripts are rational. You will do this by comparing your thoughts and scripts against rational criteria to make decisions about whether or not a thought or script is rational. You will also learn to develop and apply questions that will serve as "rational filters" for screening out thoughts that do not measure up to rationality.

In the most basic epistemology, rational thoughts, Life Scripts, and actions should be based on objective truth and logic. However, because not everyone's logic is actually logical, it helps to add some additional criteria when differentiating between rational and irrational thoughts, Life Scripts, and actions.

Generally speaking, behavioral scientists and cognitive-behavioral therapists agree on a number of factors that characterize rational thoughts. Most agree that for a thought to be rational it must 1) help you develop and sustain a rational self-identity; 2) be logical and consistent with known facts and reality—based on truth; 3) produce desired emotions; 4) help overcome current and future problems; 5) encourage serenity, personal growth, development, and happiness; 6) encourage learning from the past, preparing for the future, and living in the present; 7) support personal and interpersonal goals; and 8) support an optimistic view of one's self and future.

Conversely, if a thought you are thinking 1) causes you to form an irrational sense of self-identity; 2) is not logical and/or there is no evidence to support it as true; 3) does not help you feel the way you want to feel; 4) does not help you overcome your problems; 5) is destructive to yourself or others; and/or 6) undermines your goals, it's irrational.

As is the case with rational thoughts, rational actions can be further clarified with some specific criteria. Accordingly, rational actions are behaviors that 1) have a basis in reality to support their intended effects; 2) contribute to health, personal growth, and emotional maturity; 3) increase happiness; 4) help you feel the way you want to feel; and 5) help you achieve your goals. As with irrational thinking, actions that 1) are not logical or evidence based; 2) undermine your health and wellbeing, 3) decrease happiness and serenity, 4) do not help you feel the way you want to feel; and/or 5) do not help you solve your problems or achieve your goals, are considered irrational.

Finally, because Life Scripts are the sum total of the thoughts we think and the stories we tell ourselves to make sense of these thoughts, it follows that thinking and acting rationally is evidence of what I call "Rational Life Scripts." Conversely, it's obvious that those who hold irrational beliefs, think irrational thoughts, and behave irrationally are being directed by irrational Life Scripts, which are the focal point of Life Script Restructuring.

Taken together, rational thoughts, Life Scripts, and actions translate into what I refer to as rational living. This means that any time you increase your rational thinking, Life Scripts, or actions, you are increasing your overall rationality. This is important because, based on everything I have observed in my clinics and population interventions and research, there is a direct correlation between increased rationality and happiness. In other words, if you increase your rational living, you will experience increased happiness and an overall sense of well-being. Because being happy is more rational than being unhappy, the LSR process assumes that all thoughts, Life Scripts, and actions that increase life satisfaction are labeled "rational." Whereas, thoughts, Life Scripts, and actions that reduce life satisfaction are classified as "irrational" because they reduce happiness, serenity, and a sense of well-being.

ACT I
DETERMINING WHAT YOU WANT AS A BASIS FOR IDENTIFYING IRRATIONAL LIFE SCRIPTS AND WRITING NEW ONES

In his book, The 7 Habits of Highly Effective People, Steven Covey admonished his readers to "Begin with the end in mind." In keeping with this incredibly simple and, at the same time, incredibly important concept, the first ACT in the Life Script Restructuring (LSR) process is to help you determine your personal goals and vision in life as a basis for determining whether or not your Life Scripts will logically help you achieve your goals and realize your vision. To this end, this ACT will help you develop a Rational Personal Vision Statement and set rational goals.

CREATING A RATIONAL PERSONAL VISION STATEMENT

As a first step toward clarifying the life you want to live, it's helpful to develop a Rational Personal Vision Statement (RPVS). When completed, your RPVS will represent a rational (based on objective truth), optimistic, broad-based, mental model of your highest and best self and of a bright and promising future.

As you will notice, as I explain the purpose and actions required to complete this step, I will consistently use words like "see" and "visualize." This is because this step and the steps that follow include a number of activities that tap into the right side of your brain, the hemisphere of your brain attributed to creativity. Ultimately, as you begin to understand the techniques outlined in ACT IV, these right-brain activities will make this ACT and the entire LSR process more efficient and effective.

There are many benefits to developing an RPVS. For example, because your RPVS will articulate what your "ideal" self and life will look like, it will be easier to develop the goals and Life Scripts that will help you to realize your vision. An RPVS can also serve as a yardstick against which you can measure your current situation and your progress after you write and implement your new Life Scripts.

Unlike a goal, once you have created it, your RPVS will rarely change. This is because it represents the very essence of who you are, who you want to become, and your reasons (your "WHYs") for the way you want to experience and see yourself and your future. In short, you are manufacturing a new perspective. When you adopt this new perspective, you will start to notice that your thoughts, Life Scripts, and actions will begin to align with this new outlook which, in turn, will help you begin to leave behind your old, irrational ways of thinking and acting.

For obvious and rational reasons, your RPVS should have a positive tone. This is because the way you see yourself and your future impacts everything you think and do. Above all, it impacts your level of happiness and sense of serenity.

If your vision of self and your future is depicted in negative ways, your thoughts, behaviors, and state of happiness will be impacted negatively. Conversely, if you choose to think or do things that cause you to see yourself and your future in more positive ways (e.g., rationally viewing your future as promising and yourself as someone who has potential), your state of happiness and serenity will be influenced in a positive direction.

This is the basis for labeling a negative vision of yourself or your future as irrational. Any effort you put into seeing yourself and your potential in a more positive light is a rational decision that will lead to increased happiness and success. Lasting happiness only comes to those who think and do what it takes to attain an image of themselves and their future that is rational. This image increases, rather than diminishes, their sense of happiness, serenity, and overall success in life.

In addition to struggling with unhappiness, individuals who have an irrational view of themselves and their future (irrational Life Scripts) have trouble achieving their goals because they are held back by their thinking, their perceived abilities, and their overall potential. According to self-image psychology, to do certain things, you must see yourself as someone who can do those types of things. And, to see yourself doing certain things, you must become the kind of person who does those things. With this in mind, the purpose of this step is to help you overcome and change limiting beliefs and Life Scripts about yourself, your abilities, and your future potential by creating an RPVS that will enable you to become the kind of person who does the kinds of things you want to do in life.

We become what we want to be by consistently being what we want to become. Character is a manifestation of what you are becoming.
- Richard G. Scott

I have successfully used the techniques described in this step to help both my therapy and coaching clients 1) identify irrational beliefs and Life Scripts about themselves and their future that limit their potential and 2) replace these irrational beliefs with a Rational Personal Vision Statement (a mental prototype of how individuals view themselves and their future) and corresponding Life Scripts that give them a sense of hope and promise regarding themselves and their potential. This step will help you begin manufacturing and testing your RPVS as a means of deciding how you want and need to see yourself to achieve your full potential and, act as a basis for evaluating your new, rational Life Scripts (logical, constructive internal narratives) developed in ACT III.

As you begin this process it is useful to remember that the objective here is to design a prototype RPVS that represents the best possible person you can become (given the real, instead of the perceived, limits on your potential) while living the best possible life you can live. In other words, the RPVS you develop and evaluate should represent what you want to become, do, feel, think, own, associate with, and impact by some date in the future.

There are several steps involved in designing and testing a Rational Personal Vision Statement (RPVS). These steps include the following:

1) Ask yourself the following "Visioning Questions" to help you begin thinking about what you want to put into your RPVS:

- What inspires me? What do I want my life to stand for?

- If I could fix one problem in the world what would it be? What would I do about this problem?

- What are my most important values?

- What are the main things that motivate me/bring me joy and satisfaction?

- What are the two best moments I have experienced in the past 10 years?

- What three things would I do if I won a 200 million dollar lottery?

- What are my greatest strengths/abilities/traits/things I do best?

- What are at least two things I can start doing/do more often that use my strengths and bring me joy?

- What are at least two things I can start thinking that will bring me greater happiness?

- What are at least two things I would like to stop doing or do as little as possible?

- If a miracle occurred and my life was just as I wanted it to be, what would be different?

2) Use the "Rational Personal Vision Statement Guide" to a) identify pictures or images that represent the things you want to BEcome, Do, or Get—taken together, these images will represent your ideal RPVS; b) briefly explain how each image represents something you want; c) describe the reason "WHY" you want these things; and d) after you have described what you want and WHY, decide on one "Cue Word" that represents each of the images making up your RPVS.

3) Use the "RPVS Rationality Guide" to evaluate and identify elements in your RPVS that are irrational.

4) Revise the irrational elements in your RPVS.

5) Repeat steps 2 and 3 until all elements in your RPVS are rational.

Rational Personal Vision Statement Guide

Identify 10 pictures or images that represent what you want to **BE, DO, GET**. After you have finished this step, these images will represent your Rational Personal Vision Statement. Briefly 1) explain how each image represents something you want to **BE** (calm, successful, thin, on time, confident, faithful, disciplined, fun, trustworthy, etc.), **DO** (graduate from college, get married, travel around the world, write a book, etc.) and **GET** (a new car or home, great job, a boat, etc.). Then describe the reason WHY you want the things represented by each picture. After you have described how you want to see yourself and your future, and WHY, decide on 1 "Cue-Word" that represents each of the images making up your PVS.

| IMAGE 1 | I want to... | The reasons WHY are... | Cue Word 1 |

| IMAGE 2 | I want to... | The reasons WHY are... | Cue Word 2 |

| IMAGE 3 | I want to... | The reasons WHY are... | Cue Word 3 |

| IMAGE 4 | I want to... | The reasons WHY are... | Cue Word 4 |

| IMAGE 5 | I want to... | The reasons WHY are... | Cue Word 5 |

| IMAGE 6 | I want to... | The reasons WHY are... | Cue Word 6 |

| IMAGE 7 | I want to... | The reasons WHY are... | Cue Word 7 |

| IMAGE 8 | I want to... | The reasons WHY are... | Cue Word 8 |

| IMAGE 9 | I want to... | The reasons WHY are... | Cue Word 9 |

| IMAGE 10 | I want to... | The reasons WHY are... | Cue Word 10 |

RPVS Rationality Guide

Ask each element (represented by an image and cue word) in your initial Rational Personal Vision Statement (RPVS) the following questions. If you answer no to any of these questions it's likely that the element you are considering is irrational. Revise the irrational elements until you can answer yes to every question. Feel free to add to or take away from the questions provided here.

If I fully adopt this element in my Rational Personal Vision Statement, will I:

- reach my full potential?
- become the kind of person I want to be?
- achieve my short- and long-term goals?
- learn from my past, prepare for my future, and live in the present?
- have the ability to think and act in terms of principles and not emotions?
- perceive myself as someone who is in control of my destiny?
- be able to solve my problems and ask others for help when I need it?
- feel secure about who I am, and not feel insecure when others question how I see myself and live my life?
- be able to evaluate what others think and feel against my own standards, and have the courage to act according to my own convictions, regardless of what others do or say?
- feel secure enough about my beliefs that I can change them in the face of new facts?
- be able to exercise self-control by stoping, thinking, and making rational decisions?
- look beyond the surface, find real meaning, and weigh the pros and cons of an event or issue?
- wait for things that I want even when this requires patience and delaying immediate gratification?
- keep trying, even when things don't go the way I would like them to?
- see myself as someone who is equal in value to others, rather than inferior or superior, while accepting differences in my abilities, socio-economic standing, and personal potential?
- respect and obey the laws that are rational in that they are fair and just?
- respect the dignity of all men and women, without respect to religion, race, or gender?

SETTING RATIONAL GOALS

After doing what it takes to develop a Rational Personal Vision Statement, you can begin to apply your RPVS by 1) setting a single goal for each RPVS element, 2) evaluating the rationality of your goals, and 3) determining whether or not you are ready to achieve the goals you plan to set. All of this can be accomplished in the following steps:

1) Use the "RPVS Goal Guide" that follows to write down at least one goal for each element in your RPVS. These goals are essentially written statements that explain what you want to obtain or accomplish within a certain period of time. They should be specific, measurable, realistic, and stated in terms of a specific time period.

2) For each goal you set using the "RPVS Goal Guide," ask yourself the following questions:

- Do I believe I can achieve this goal?

- Do I have what it takes to achieve the goal (e.g., knowledge, skills, resources, support)?

- Based on my responses to the last question, what do I need to think or do to get what I need to accomplish each goal?

- To assess and begin building your motivation to achieve each goal, ask yourself these questions:

- Why do I want to achieve this particular goal?

- What good things may happen if I achieve this goal?

• What bad things may happen if I do not reach this goal?

• How will things be different if I achieve this goal?

4) (a) To further assess your readiness (including how committed you are, how confident you are, and how prepared you are), you can ask yourself the following questions for each goal:

How committed am I that I can achieve this goal? (circle number)

(no commitment) 0 -- 1 -- 2 -- 3 -- 4 -- 5 -- 6 -- 7 -- 8 -- 9 -- 10 (totally committed)

How confident am I that I can achieve this goal? (circle number)

(no confidence) 0 -- 1 -- 2 -- 3 -- 4 -- 5 -- 6 -- 7 -- 8 -- 9 -- 10 (totally confident)

How prepared am I to achieve this goal? (circle number)

(no preparation) 0 -- 1 -- 2 -- 3 -- 4 -- 5 -- 6 -- 7 -- 8 -- 9 -- 10 (totally prepared)

4) (b) What do you need to raise each number you circled to a 10?

5) What else do you need to achieve the goal? Improved self-image, knowledge, skills, social support, money?

RPVS Goal Guide

Use this form to write down at least one goal for each element in your Rational Personal Vision Statement (RPVS). Be precise and only include goals that you are committed to, confident that you can attain, and are congruent with your RPVS.
CUE 1
CUE 2
CUE 3
CUE 4
CUE 5
CUE 6
CUE 7
CUE 8
CUE 9
CUE 10

Finally, the work you have done in ACT I is designed to help you understand what you really want in life. Now that you have a good idea, based on your RPVS and your corresponding goals, it's time to move forward with ACT II where you will begin to systematically identify your irrational Life Scripts that have been and will continue to, if they are not restructured, undermine your ability to achieve your goals and realize your vision.

ACT II
IDENTIFYING IRRATIONAL LIFE SCRIPTS

Our conscious mind has a voice. This is evident because as humans, we talk to ourselves inside—all of the time. It is how we know what we are thinking and feeling. In fact, as I stated earlier, it's been estimated that the average adult thinks between 20,000 and 70,000 thoughts per day.

According to a number of personality psychologists, to make sense out of the thousands of thoughts we think each day we organize them into "narratives" and "life stories" (McAdams, 2001). I call these stories Life Scripts because, like scripts used to direct actors in a play, these conscious and subconscious stories direct everything we say and do across our life span. If the thoughts you currently think and the stories you tell yourself to explain these thoughts do not align with the kind of life you want to live as identified in ACT I, you can readily label these as irrational based on the criteria of Rationality discussed in the Prologue. In addition to your irrational Life Scripts that don't line up with your RPVS and goals, it's quite likely that you have many other, not so obvious, thoughts and stories that you tell yourself that can also be classified as irrational Life Scripts.

The purpose of this step is to help you identify upsetting thoughts and stories that you tell yourself that are causing preventable problems and that are associated with emotional distress, undermine your ability to cope rationally, and prevent you from achieving your potential. These irrational thoughts and life stories (Life Scripts) become the focal point of ACT III where you will systematically edit and/or replace the irrational Life Scripts identified in ACT II.

I have provided you with three means of systematically identifying irrational Life Scripts. The first approach relies on an adapted version of Erik Erikson's Theory of Psychosocial Development, taken together with a number of relevant questions, to help you identify irrational Life Scripts across eight stages of life. The second approach guides you in a process of comparing your current beliefs and thoughts against irrational beliefs identified by prominent psychologist, Albert Ellis, as those that tend to spawn irrational thinking. This comparison will help you identify irrational beliefs that you currently hold that make up your irrational Life Scripts. Finally, the third approach provides you with some direction that will help you consider how your "roles" and relationships across your life have resulted in maladaptive patterns that are currently represented by irrational Life Scripts.

A THEORY FOR FRAMING ACT II

The father of social psychology, Kurt Lewin (Lewin, 1952, p. 169), once said: "There is nothing more practical than a good theory." I believe this to be true because a good theory, even though it represents the probable and the possible but not necessarily the actual, can provide a useful framework for understanding human development, thought, and behavior. With this in mind, I have adapted Erik Erikson's Theory of Psychosocial Development (Erikson, 1963; Erikson, 1968) for the purpose of helping you systematically identify irrational Life Scripts across eight life stages of your life span.

The reason I chose this theory over other prominent developmental theories by Piaget (Piaget, 1972), Vygotsky (Vygotsky, 1978), or Kohlberg (Kohlberg, 1979), for example, is because Erikson's work gets to the heart of psychosocial experiences that make up the unpleasant memories and stories (McAdams, 2001) that individuals tell themselves that cause them to emotionally struggle. I also want to make clear that I do not agree with everything Erikson postulated in his theory. This is mostly due to the fact that it's difficult to examine transitions through life stages under controlled conditions and, because of this, there is very little convincing empirical evidence to support his theory, including how individuals transition from one stage to the next or how one resolves a crisis within a stage.

I also understand that there are many limitations connected with relying on a single theory like Erikson's and that, because of these limitations, many researchers have adopted a trans-theoretical approach to conceptualizing and updating how they think about human development. That is, rather than relying on one theory, they choose among the most salient factors or features of prominent, well-grounded theories for a given situation. However, in doing so they can lose the benefits of the structure provided by a theoretical model. Hence, the trade-off for inflexibility is a loss of structure provided by a theoretical paradigm. Because I am unwilling to make this trade-off, and because Erikson's ideas fit with my research, clinical experiences, and the purposes of this book, I continue to rely on this theory as a framework for helping others systematically identify psychosocial Life Scripts that work for or against them.

One last point before describing how you can apply Erikson's theory to LSR is the fact that as a consequence of his conjectures about human behavior and development, Erikson, in effect, invented a number of diseases that he neglected to invent cures for. This is a lighthearted way of saying that even though Erikson's work is important and useful, it's just a theory that, once again, represents something reasonably close to, but not actually, the truth. This is where the LSR process comes into play in that it allows you to apply an inductive process to a very prominent deductive theory to determine whether or not your experiences across time line up with, or in some way deviate from, the thinking of a leading theorist like Erikson. It may also help you discover how you did or did not effectively transition from one psychosocial stage of development to the next. And, if you did not successfully resolve the conflicts in the stages of Erikson's model, the LSR process will help you begin to discover why and how you can go back and resolve unsuccessful or maladaptive transitions across your life span.

Using The Psychosocial Development Theory to Identify Irrational Life Scripts

Erik Erikson's psychosocial theory of human development asserts that, across a full life span from infancy to late adulthood, all humans must transition through eight successive psychosocial stages (See Column 1, Table 1). Each stage is associated with specific types of biological and psychosocial challenges that must be mastered to ensure successful outcomes and avoid the problems associated with "arrested development" in later stages. These crises (Erikson, 1963; McLeod, 2013) are psychosocial in nature because they involve the psychological needs of the individual (i.e., psycho) conflicting with the needs and pressures of society (i.e., social expectations and norms).

Favorable stage-specific outcomes tend to increase the likelihood of successfully completing subsequent stages and result in a healthier personality, a more positive sense of self, an increased ability to successfully relate to others, and more rational thoughts and actions overall. Successful outcomes across each stage are illustrated in Column 4 of Table 1. This column includes "Character Virtues and Positive Outcomes" in the form of brief descriptions that characterize individuals who successfully navigate each stage of development.

Unhealthy outcomes tend to result in a diminished ability to complete further stages, an unhealthy sense of self, and more difficulty relating to others. Brief examples of these unhealthy outcomes can be seen in Column 5 of Table 1.

Table 1
Summary of Erikson's Theory of Psychosocial Development

Approximate Age	Psycho-Social Crisis	Existential Question
Infancy birth–18 months	Basic Trust vs. Mistrust	Can I trust the world?
Early Childhood (Toddler) 2-3 years	Autonomy vs. Shame and Doubt	Is it okay to be me?
Preschool 4-5 years	Initiative vs. Guilt	Is it okay for me to do, move, and act?

Table 1
Summary of Erikson's Theory of Psychosocial Development

Character Virtues & Positive Outcomes	Negative Outcomes (Arrested Development)
Hope as evidenced by being "grounded" with a sense of security and inner calm, trusting in self and others. Having a sense that everything will work out no matter how difficult things get. An inner resolve and resilience in the face of risk and adversity. Hope and faith in the future and one's place in it. Trust in the environment. Believing that others are dependable and reliable.	**Insecure.** Not securely attached. Suspicious and fearful of others and the future. Anxious, defensive, aggressive, and/or unsympathetic. Little enthusiasm. A lack of persistence. An underlying belief that the world is conspiring against oneself.
Willpower evidenced by self-control, discipline, self-determination, self-reliance, confidence in decision making, persistence, independent thinking, and a sense of responsibility. Self-sufficiency, self-confidence, self-control, a sense of adequacy, and independence.	**Lack of independence,** self-doubt, feelings of inadequacy and shame, low self-efficacy (i.e., the perception that one has the ability to cope with a situation or apply one's skills to cope or accomplish a task).
Purpose evidenced by a sense of independent thinking, independent decision making, initiating projects, cooperating with others, guiding others, taking initiative and calculated risks. Guilt free when using one's imagination. Ability to be a self-starter and to initiate one's own activities.	**Guilt** related to personal thoughts and actions, including one's perceived failures. Feelings of inadequacy. Afraid to try new things for fear of failing. The belief that one can't do things by oneself. Lack of independence. Hesitant to do things alone. Worried about what others will think. Thinking "I can't do it alone," or that doing things on one's own is "not OK." Inhibition to move forward because of guilt and fear of being punished because of failure.

Table 1
Summary of Erikson's Theory of Psychosocial Development

Approximate Age	Psycho-Social Crisis	Existential Question
School Age 6-11 years	Industry vs. Inferiority	Can I make it in the world of people and things?
Adolescence 12-18 years	Identity vs. Role Confusion	Who am I and what can I become?
Young Adult 19-39 years	Intimacy vs. Isolation	Can I love?

Table 1
Summary of Erikson's Theory of Psychosocial Development

Character Virtues & Positive Outcomes	Negative Outcomes (Arrested Development)
Competence evidenced by contributing, making things, learning and applying new skills, confidence in one's ability to contribute, pursuing goals, feeling capable of contributing. Ability to learn how things work, to understand, and to organize. Discovering pleasure in being productive and being successful. Enjoying intellectual stimulation.	**A sense of inferiority.** Failing at a task results in frustration and feelings of inadequacy. Low self-efficacy evidenced by a lack of confidence in one's ability to use personal skills to cope with the rigors of life or accomplish a task. No sense of mastery.
Fidelity evidenced by a coherent self-concept and a growing sense of personal identity and esteem, visualizing a useful role and purpose in life, self-confidence, personal standards and boundaries, social allegiance, discipline and discretion, pride, and personal identity. Seeing one's self as a unique and integrated person that has a role to play in the world, both in the present and the future.	**Confusion** over who and what one really is. Inability to identify a satisfactory or appropriate path or role in life. Uncertainty about how personal knowledge, skills, and abilities can be applied in a way that is meaningful in the present and/or the future. Lack of personal insight and appreciation for self and one's role in the world. No sense of having a legitimate place in the present or future. The belief that the world is conspiring against oneself.
Love evidenced by the ability to give and receive love, developing and maintaining intimate emotional and physical connections with others, forming lasting reciprocating relationships and friendships, including positive relationships at work and in one's personal life. Ability to make and keep commitments to others.	**Inability to form affectionate relationships.** Fear of relationships with others. Feelings of isolation and aloneness. Fear of commitment. Difficulty making and sustaining long-term relationships with one or more individuals. Unable to depend on others.

Table 1
Summary of Erikson's Theory of Psychosocial Development

Approximate Age	Psycho-Social Crisis	Existential Question
Middle Adult 40-64 years	Generativity vs. Stagnation	Can I make my life count?
Older Adult 65-death	Ego Integrity vs. Despair	Is it okay to have been me?

Table 1
Summary of Erikson's Theory of Psychosocial Development

Character Virtues & Positive Outcomes	Negative Outcomes (Arrested Development)
Caring as evidenced by unconditional love for children and family members, support and sacrifice for children, concern and voluntary service to others and the community, "thinking globally and acting locally," trying to make a difference in the world, building a legacy. Altruism demonstrated by an unselfish concern for the welfare of others, sacrificing to help others through a crisis or demanding situation or period in their life.	**Concerned only for self, one's own well-being, and prosperity.** Caught up in a self-centered lifestyle. A halt in personal growth or a sense of stagnation in life. No sense of contribution evidenced by trivializing one's activities. The inability to conceive oneself as a productive member of society.
Wisdom as evidenced by serenity, tolerance, reconciling regrets, accepting the inevitability of physical decline and death, imparting life lessons to posterity, peace of mind, spiritual reflection, and reconciliation, accepting loss and the departure of friends and family. A sense of integrity and fulfillment, and a willingness to face death.	**Dissatisfaction with life.** A sense of despair. Many regrets about the past and lost opportunities. Refusal to consider having made a meaningful contribution in the past. Lack of hope. Consumed with a sense of bitterness and despair regarding the future. A fear of death.

One of the main elements of Erikson's theory that is most useful in Act II of LSR is his focus on the development of personal identity (Sokol, 2009). Your identity is your conscious sense of self that is developed through your life experiences and interactions with others. It includes your beliefs, personal standards, and values that help shape and guide your thoughts and actions in the here and now.

Because you begin experiencing and interacting with your environment and others at birth, the formation of your identity begins in childhood and continues throughout your life. This identity is recorded in your mind in the form of thoughts, life stories (McAdams, 2001), and Life Scripts that help you make sense of the world and your place in it. These scripts can be labeled as rational or irrational, depending on their defining characteristics. For example, if your Life Scripts about who you are and the role you "should" play in your world are to be considered as rational, they must 1) help you develop and sustain a rational self-identity; 2) be logical and consistent with known facts and reality—based on truth; 3) produce desired emotions; 4) help overcome current and future problems; 5) encourage serenity, personal growth, development, and happiness; 6) encourage learning from the past, preparing for the future, and living in the present; 7) support personal and interpersonal goals; and 8) support an optimistic view of one's self and future. If, on the other hand, your Life Scripts 1) cause you to form an irrational sense of self identity; 2) are not logical and/or there is no evidence to support their truth; 3) do not help you feel the way you want to feel; 4) do not help you overcome your problems; 5) do not promote feelings of serenity, 6) are destructive to yourself or others; and/or 7) undermine your goals and your ability to become your highest and best self, they are irrational and will cause you any number of problems until they are either edited or rewritten completely into cohesive Life Scripts that support a rational, healthy life.

Another important aspect of Erikson's theory that is applicable to the LSR process is his belief that individuals who are able to successfully navigate the challenges in a stage of their development will gain a sense of competence and self-mastery that will help them navigate successive stages (Marcia, 1993). From the perspective of LSR, this sense of competence helps individuals internalize Life Scripts that support and motivate rational thoughts and actions. At the same time, when developmental stages are not handled well, individuals will not gain the confidence required to successfully navigate future stages and will, as I mentioned earlier, experience a form of arrested psychosocial development. In the LSR context, this means many of the Life Scripts of those who do not successfully resolve a crisis in one or more life stages will include irrational story lines that, when repeated over and over again, produce a sense of inadequacy that, in turn, undermines one's ability to be happy and okay when things in life are not okay.

One of the most promising aspects of Erikson's theory in the context of ACT II in the LSR process is the work Erikson and others have done (Erikson, 1968; Marcia, 1993) to demonstrate that unresolved conflicts across stages can be resolved at a later time. In other words, if a person initially dealt with a particular life-stage challenge in a maladaptive way, he or she can take steps to identify the unresolved challenges and then work to resolve these challenges in a way that results in a better state of well-being.

In fact, relatively recent discoveries in neuroscience regarding brain neuroplasticity (Cole, 2013) provide strong evidence that there is plenty of room for continued growth and development throughout one's life span. Because LSR relies heavily on leveraging brain plasticity, if applied as outlined across the four LSR ACTS, it will readily help you identify what is holding you back so that you can almost immediately begin to experience new and ongoing growth and development in areas of your life where you have been stuck because of arrested development in an earlier life stage. Specifically, as was alluded to above, this process involves identifying upsetting Life Scripts across the life stages and then changing these scripts in a way that helps you successfully resolve previously unresolved life-stage conflicts.

For example, ACT II will help you identify upsetting Life Scripts and unresolved conflicts across each life stage. ACT III will help you resolve the conflicts by "restructuring" the maladaptive Life Scripts identified in ACT II. ACT IV will help you maintain your change toward a happier, healthier personality by helping you manipulate neural pathways in a way that makes your "path of least resistance" a super highway toward becoming your highest and best self.

IDENTIFYING UPSETTING STORIES AT EACH STAGE OF DEVELOPMENT

With the understanding that the purpose of ACT II is to help you identify irrational Life Scripts in the context of Erikson's conceptual framework, I have provided you with a number of questions that are designed to help you get to the root causes of your irrational Life Scripts across each stage in your past. These questions include the "existential questions" in Column 3 of Table 1, questions related to Character Virtues and Positive Outcomes described in Column 4, and Negative Outcomes outlined in Column 5. I have also included questions related to both vicarious and personal memories and related stories. By vicarious, I mean the memories and stories related by individuals whom you know who have insights into your life stages that you were too young to recall. This information is necessary because you will not have conscious memories of early stages of your development. Hence, individuals who knew you during these stages can help you "fill in the apparent blanks" and even trigger memories that you have forgotten.

All of these questions are designed to help you remember upsetting memories, identify the thoughts that go along with each memory, document the stories you tell yourself to make sense of these thoughts, and then attempt to identify the negative emotions that go along with these thoughts and memories. Negative emotions can include feeling embarrassed, guilty, angry, outraged, sad, incompetent, afraid, anxious, hopeless, unhappy, nervous, disappointed, pessimistic, frustrated, regretful, lonely, inferior, panicky, and worthless.

If there is some truth to Erikson's theory, and I believe there is, the questions you answer may also help you gain insight into whether or not you may have dealt with a particular psychosocial crisis in a maladaptive manner. And, if yes, you can begin to target memories in the stage(s) that you did not navigate successfully.

As you will discover, these questions will help you begin to flesh out the irrational Life Scripts that create upsetting and negative emotions. Based on my clinical experience, this process will also begin to bring to mind unconscious stories that are playing under the surface. As these unconscious thoughts and stories begin to surface, you will experience any number of triggers and emotions that will help you begin to piece together what is causing the upset you have experienced. It's important that you try to capture with a recorder or some other means of documenting these ideas as they flow out of your heart and mind.

You can complete this process on your own or with the help of a trusted friend, family member, or a trained professional. Notice when I say friend or family member, I use the word trusted. This is because it's important that you feel safe when you are talking out loud about upsetting memories of your past. It's also important because your friend or family member must agree to not share, under any circumstances, what you tell them. Frankly, because it's sometimes hard to find such individuals, you may want to complete this process on your own or with a professional counselor or psychotherapist who is bound to confidentiality.

If you decide to involve another person, explain that his or her role is to ask you the questions under each stage and take notes that you will use to begin to piece together your upsetting Life Scripts. Explain that his or her role is that of a kind, concerned, compassionate parent. Also explain that what you say must be held confidential unless, of course, you do not mind if he or she shares with others your upsetting thoughts and stories.

However, even if you "don't care" at the moment someone interviews you, it's possible that you will care later. To ensure safety, you may actually prefer complete confidentiality.

Because this person will obviously have a different vantage point than what you have on the memories and stories you identify here, it's quite possible that he or she will be able to provide you useful insights into what you share. Encourage this input.

If you do not want to use a professional and/or if you do not feel safe with others and want to keep this information to yourself, simply begin answering the questions under each development stage that you have traversed. Do your best to record as much detail as you can around the memories. These details will be important as you attempt to understand the causes of your upsets and accurately lay out the patterns revealed by your upsetting thoughts and stories.

As you answer the questions in each stage, remember to be compassionate toward yourself. Without self-compassion, it will be difficult to be objective about what you uncover. This is because when you focus on memories, the ones that are embedded with heavy emotion (sometimes called "hot memories") tend to obscure important details related to the events, environment, and individuals who make up the memory. If, when you experience hot memories, you turn on yourself and blame yourself for the content of these memories, your ability to objectively capture the details and true essence of the memory will be compromised. The unchecked emotions that you generate when you turn on yourself will blur the facts of a situation and cause you to have irrational thoughts and outsized reactions around a particular memory or Life Script.

Hence, you will be unable to do the work you need to do in Act III, where you rewrite the script so that it is rational and effective in helping you move forward.

> . . . there's a story behind everything. How a
> picture got on a wall. How a scar got on your face.
> Sometimes the stories are simple, and sometimes
> they are hard and heartbreaking. But behind all
> your stories is always your mother's story, because
> hers is where yours begins.
> - Mitch Albom, For One More Day

If, during this process, you do come across memories that are encapsulated with sounds, smells, bodily sensations, and great emotional pain, you may need to get professional help. This is particularly true if you begin to experience flashbacks during the day or nightmares during the night that persist over time. Although you should expect some upsetting dreams and intense emotions as you go back and uncover the past, flashbacks or nightmares that stay with you and become increasingly upsetting may be caused by Acute- or Post-Traumatic Stress Disorder. The good news here is that the professional counseling community now has very good treatments for ASD and PTSD. Seeking out these treatments is essential to recovering from these debilitating disorders.

STAGE 1: INFANCY

The first stage of Erikson's theory of psychosocial development is called Infancy. The age range, psychosocial crisis, existential question, and character virtues described for possible healthy and unhealthy outcomes at this stage are laid out in Columns 1-5 in Table 1a. If you look at Erikson's early writing, you will note that I have adjusted the age range for this stage from 0-1 year to birth to 18 months. This age span and its interpretation are more consistent with what I have observed in my own research and clinical experience.

Table 1a

Summary of Erikson's Theory of Psychosocial Development

Approximate Age	Psycho-Social Crisis	Existential Question
Infancy birth-18 months	Basic Trust vs. Mistrust	Can I trust the world?

Character Virtues & Positive Outcomes	Negative Outcomes (Arrested Development)
Hope as evidenced by being "grounded" with a sense of security and inner calm, trusting in self and others. Having a sense that everything will work out no matter how difficult things get. An inner resolve and resilience in the face of risk and adversity. Hope and faith in the future and one's place in it. Trust in the environment. Believing that others are dependable and reliable.	**Insecure.** Not securely attached. Suspicious and fearful of others and the future. Anxious, defensive, aggressive, and/or unsympathetic. Little enthusiasm. A lack of persistence. An underlying belief that the world is conspiring against oneself.

This is the stage when you were utterly dependent on your caretaker (typically your mother) for food, warmth, attention, and affection. According to this theory, if your needs were consistently met, you developed a secure attachment with your parents which, in turn, resulted in gaining a Basic Trust for your environment. Conversely, if your needs were not met during this time of dependency you did not develop trust, you became mistrusting. Failure to develop trust will result in fear and a belief that the world is inconsistent and unpredictable.

The character virtue that Erikson believes emerges in Infancy is Hope. If your needs for nourishment and love were met at this stage, you developed hope, or a sense of security.

It's very unlikely that you will have memories from this stage of your development. This is because, according to numerous studies, our first palpable recollections are typically from the age of 3 ½ years old, which is when the hippocampus (a portion of the brain used to store memories) has adequately matured to handle this task. However, if you do recall any memories, answer the following questions:

- What upsetting memories do I have during Stage 1?

- When I experience these memories, what thoughts come to mind?

- When I experience the thoughts related to these upsetting memories, what stories do I tell myself to make sense of these thoughts?

- What negative emotions do I feel when I tell myself these stories? Negative emotions can include feeling embarrassed, guilty, angry, outraged, sad, incompetent, afraid, anxious, hopeless, unhappy, nervous, disappointed, pessimistic, frustrated, regretful, lonely, inferior, panicky, and worthless.

If you do not have any memories from your first stage of development (since most people will not), I suggest that you talk to others who knew you during this stage about your life and ask them the following questions about your experiences:

- Did I have a difficult birth? If yes, how long did I stay in the hospital after birth?

- Was I attached to my mother? Was she attentive to my needs? Was she a good mother?

- Were my parents/caretakers attentive to my needs?

- Did I have any serious injuries during this time period? Was I abused in any way?

In addition to asking those who knew you during this stage of your life questions about you and your experiences, you can also gain insights into your early experiences by reading journals, looking at your baby pictures, or watching home videos.

In my case, my mother carefully compiled what she called a "Baby Book," which includes pictures of me as an infant, a lock of hair, both a hand and a footprint, a brief description of the events around my birth, the weather on the day of my birth, the name and some information about the physician who delivered me, etc. As I recently went through this book, everything in it seemed so far away and yet so familiar. One picture of my grandfather holding me on the back of a young palomino quarter horse popped out, and for a second, it was as if I could remember the event. I do know the event had a profound impact on me because, to this day, I still own and love to ride quarter horses even though I live in a large city.

Do not be surprised if the information you gain from reflecting on the above questions related to your Infancy (as related to you by your chosen informers and/or as gathered from your response to the existential question that follows) begins to unlock unconscious memories. When you do experience new memories, record them. They may help you recall other memories from later stages of your life.

You may also want to reflect on whether or not you are a trusting person, given that Stage 1 is the phase in our lives, according to Erikson, when we deal with the crisis of Trust versus Mistrust. To gain some idea of whether or not Erikson's theory applies to you, answer the following existential question and then compare your answer with the other information you have collected about this stage of your development.

Generally speaking, do I trust the world around me?

I do not trust anyone or anything   1...2...3...4...5...6...7...8...9...10   I am one of the most trusting people I know

Obviously, if you are mostly mistrusting and if you, in turn, hear stories about your Infancy that indicate that your caregivers were not attentive or that you basic needs were not met, and/or that you had an extended stay in the hospital, this correlation between mistrust and your negative experiences during infancy will give you some insight into why you currently have trouble trusting others.

Signs that you may not have successfully navigated this stage of your development are referenced in Column 4 of Table 1a. Similarly, indications that you did not have a safe, secure environment during your infancy are laid out in Column 5 in the same table.

Finally, given the positive and negative outcomes explained in Columns 4 and 5 in Table 1a, I have provided you with some questions related to these outcomes as they correspond with this stage. These questions will help you gain insight into your own development and may also trigger memories or Life Scripts that have bearing on your present thoughts, emotions, attitudes, and actions. The questions are framed in a way that will help you think about whether or not you have experienced a positive or negative outcome related to the constructs discussed under this stage of development. The questions are as follows:

- Do I have hope and faith in the future and my place in it?

- Do I have a sense that everything will work out no matter how difficult things get in my life or in the world in general?

- Do I have inner resolve and resilience in the face of adversity?

- Do I believe others are mostly dependable and reliable?

Based on your answers to these questions, use the following table or your journal to record personal insights. As is depicted in the table, one useful way of organizing these epiphanies is to record upsetting memories that you identified during this stage. Once these are recorded, you can then begin to piece together the irrational Life Scripts that you repeat to make sense of these memories. As a reminder of this process, this table will be included at the end of each of the eight stage-specific questions.

STAGE 1 INSIGHTS

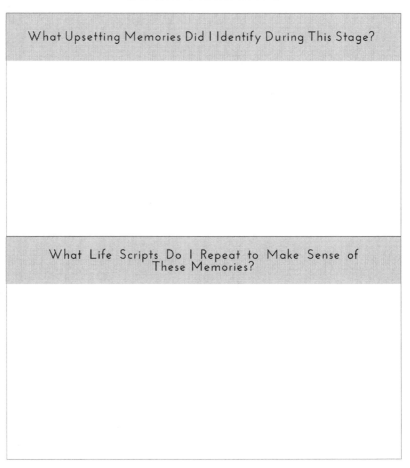

What Upsetting Memories Did I Identify During This Stage?
What Life Scripts Do I Repeat to Make Sense of These Memories?

STAGE 2: EARLY CHILDHOOD (TODDLER)

The second stage of Erikson's theory of psychosocial development is called Early Childhood or Toddler. Once again, the age range, psychosocial crisis, existential question, and character virtues described for possible healthy and unhealthy outcomes at this stage are laid out in Columns 1-5, in Table 1b.

Table 1b

Summary of Erikson's Theory of Psychosocial Development

Approximate Age	Psycho-Social Crisis	Existential Question
Early Childhood (Toddler) 2-3 years	Autonomy vs. Shame and Doubt	Is it okay to be me?

Character Virtues & Positive Outcomes	Negative Outcomes (Arrested Development)
Willpower evidenced by self-control, discipline, self-determination, self-reliance, confidence in decision making, persistence, independent thinking, and a sense of responsibility. Self-sufficiency, self-confidence, self-control, a sense of adequacy, and independence.	**Lack of independence,** self-doubt, feelings of inadequacy and shame, low self-efficacy (i.e., the perception that one has the ability to cope with a situation or apply one's skills to cope or accomplish a task).

From ages 2-3, you began learning how to do things for yourself. During this stage you learned to walk, assert yourself, talk, use the toilet, etc. According to Erikson, a successful developmental outcome of this stage is independence or Autonomy. This outcome is most likely to occur if your parents/caretakers encouraged you to use initiative and reassured you when you made mistakes. In such cases, it's predicted that you will develop the confidence needed to cope with future situations that require choice, control, and independence.

The character virtue gained in this stage is Will or Willpower. Evidence that you may have successfully navigated this stage is outlined in Column 4. Characteristics of someone who did not develop in a healthy way during this stage are provided in Column 5.

Once again, it's unlikely that you will have conscious, vivid memories from this stage since most people do not have memories until they are 3 ½. If you do have any memories, answer the following questions:

- What upsetting memories do I have during Stage 2?

- When I experience these memories, what thoughts come to mind?

- When I experience the thoughts related to these upsetting memories, what stories do I tell myself to make sense of these thoughts?

- What negative emotions do I feel when I tell myself these stories? Negative emotions can include feeling embarrassed, guilty, angry, outraged, sad, incompetent, afraid, anxious, hopeless, unhappy, nervous, disappointed, pessimistic, frustrated, regretful, lonely, inferior, panicky, and worthless.

If you do not have any memories from your Toddler stage of development, I suggest that you speak to others who knew you during this stage. Some stage-relevant questions you may want to ask them include:

- Were my parents overprotective? If yes, how so?

- Did they disapprove of my acts of independence?

- Did they appear to be ashamed of my behaviors?

- Did they doubt my abilities?

- Did I have a serious injury or illness during this stage that required me to be dependent on others for an extended period of time?

In addition to asking those who knew you during this stage of your life questions about you and your experiences, you can also gain insights into your Toddler experiences by reading journals, looking at pictures of yourself, or watching home videos.

Once again, the information you receive from observers of your Toddler stage may help you begin to unlock unconscious memories. Moreover, these memories may help you recall other memories from later stages of your life.

To gain some idea of whether or not Erikson's theory applies to you, answer the following existential question and then compare your answer with the other information you have collected about this stage of your development.

Generally speaking, do I believe it's okay to be me?

Not at All   1...2...3...4...5...6...7...8...9...10   Absolutely

Finally, given the positive and negative outcomes explained in Columns 4 and 5 in Table 1b, I have provided you with some questions related to these outcomes as they correspond with this stage. These questions will help you gain insight into your own development and may also trigger memories or Life Scripts that have bearing on your present thoughts, emotions, attitudes, and actions. The questions are framed in a way that will help you think about whether or not you have experienced a positive or negative outcome related to the constructs discussed under this stage of development. The questions are as follows:

• Do I have problems with self-discipline?

• Do I have problems with my self-control?

• Do I have trouble with self-reliance? In other words, am I mostly dependent on others?

• Do I have confidence in my decision making?

• Am I persistent?

• Am I an independent thinker?

• Am I self-sufficient?

STAGE 2 INSIGHTS

What Upsetting Memories Did I Identify During This Stage?

What Life Scripts Do I Repeat to Make Sense of These Memories?

STAGE 3: PRESCHOOL

The third stage of Erikson's theory of psychosocial development is called Preschool. The age range, psychosocial crisis, existential question, and character virtues described for possible healthy and unhealthy outcomes at this stage are laid out in Columns 1-5 in Table 1c.

Table 1c

Summary of Erikson's Theory of Psychosocial Development

Approximate Age	Psycho-Social Crisis	Existential Question
Preschool 4-5 years	Initiative vs. Guilt	Is it okay for me to do, move, and act?

Character Virtues & Positive Outcomes	Negative Outcomes (Arrested Development)
Purpose evidenced by a sense of independent thinking, independent decision making, initiating projects, cooperating with others, guiding others, taking initiative and calculated risks. Guilt free when using one's imagination. Ability to be a self-starter and to initiate one's own activities.	**Guilt** related to personal thoughts and actions, including one's perceived failures. Feelings of inadequacy. Afraid to try new things for fear of failing. The belief that one can't do things by oneself. Lack of independence. Hesitant to do things alone. Worried about what others will think. Thinking "I can't do it alone," or that doing things on one's own is "not OK." Inhibition to move forward because of guilt and fear of being punished because of failure.

From 3 through 5 years of age, children become increasingly engaged in social interaction with the people around them.

According to Erikson, this is the stage where you struggle with initiative versus guilt. If your caretakers taught you clear boundaries, were consistent in their discipline, accepted you when you made mistakes, and encouraged you to rebound when you experienced setbacks, you learned Initiative. You also learned to accept, without shame, that certain behaviors are not allowed. Moreover, you learned not to feel shame when using your imagination as you explored your environment and experienced your social interaction.

The character virtue gained in this stages is Purpose which, as outlined in Column 4 of Table 1c, is evidenced by those who, during this stage, successfully developed independent thinking and decision making; a proactive approach and initiative when taking on projects; willingness and ability to lead, cooperate with, and guide others; and the confidence required to take calculated risks.

Characteristics of someone who experienced arrested development at this stage are provided in Column 5 of Table 1c. According to Erikson, if you did not get the guidance and encouragement you needed at this stage, you may have developed a sense of shame. You may have also become overly reserved because of a sense of guilt and may have come to believe that it is wrong to be independent.

Although you will have few if any vivid memories during this stage, please answer the questions about the memories you do have:

• What upsetting memories do I have during Stage 3?

• When I experience these memories, what thoughts come to mind?

• When I experience the thoughts related to these upsetting memories, what stories do I tell myself to make sense of these thoughts?

• What negative emotions do I feel when I tell myself these stories? Negative emotions can include feeling embarrassed, guilty, angry, outraged, sad, incompetent, afraid, anxious, hopeless, unhappy, nervous, disappointed, pessimistic, frustrated, regretful, lonely, inferior, panicky, and worthless.

If you do not have any memories from ages 3 to 5, I suggest that you speak to others who knew you during this stage. Some stage-relevant questions you may want to ask them include:

• How did my caretakers parent me? Were they strict? Were they lenient? Were they consistent?

• Did they disapprove of my acts of independence?

• Did they punish me when I made mistakes or used my imagination?

• Did they appear to be ashamed of my behaviors?

• Did they doubt my abilities?

• Did I have a serious injury or illness during this stage that required me to be dependent on others for an extended period of time?

In addition to asking those who knew you during this stage of your life questions about you and your experiences, you can also gain insights into your experiences during your Preschool years by reading journals, looking at pictures of yourself, or watching home videos.

Once again, the information you receive from observers of your Preschool stage may help you begin to unlock unconscious memories. These memories may help you recall other memories from later stages of your life.

To gain some idea of whether or not Erikson's theory applies to you, answer the following existential question and then compare your answer with the other information you have collected about this stage of your development.

Generally speaking, is it okay for me to do, move, and act?
Not at All   1...2...3...4...5...6...7...8...9...10   Absolutely

Finally, given the positive and negative outcomes explained in Columns 4 and 5 in Table 1c, I have provided you with some questions related to these outcomes as they correspond with this stage. These questions will help you gain insight into your own development and may also trigger memories or Life Scripts that have bearing on your present thoughts, emotions, attitudes, and actions. The questions are framed in a way that will help you think about whether or not you have experienced a positive or negative outcome related to the constructs discussed under this stage of development. The questions are as follows:

- Do I have a sense of purpose in my life?

- Am I mostly an independent thinker?

• Do I tend to initiate projects or do I wait for others to start a project before I participate? In other words, am I a self-starter?

• Am I mostly proactive or reactive?

• Am I good at leading and guiding others?

• Do I feel guilty when I use my imagination?

• Am I good at cooperating with others?

STAGE 3 INSIGHTS

What Upsetting Memories Did I Identify During This Stage?
What Life Scripts Do I Repeat to Make Sense of These Memories?

STAGE 4: SCHOOL AGE

The fourth stage of Erikson's theory of psychosocial development is called School Age. The age range, psychosocial crisis, existential question, and character virtues described for possible healthy and unhealthy outcomes at this stage are laid out in Columns 1-5 in Table 1d.

Table 1d

Summary of Erikson's Theory of Psychosocial Development

Approximate Age	Psycho-Social Crisis	Existential Question
School Age 6-11 years	Industry vs. Inferiority	Can I make it in the world of people and things?

Character Virtues & Positive Outcomes		Negative Outcomes (Arrested Development)
Competence evidenced by contributing, making things, learning and applying new skills, confidence in one's ability to contribute, pursuing goals, feeling capable of contributing. Ability to learn how things work, to understand, and to organize. Discovering pleasure in being productive and being successful. Enjoying intellectual stimulation.		**A sense of inferiority.** Failing at a task results in frustration and feelings of inadequacy. Low self-efficacy evidenced by a lack of confidence in one's ability to use personal skills to cope with the rigors of life or accomplish a task. No sense of mastery.

From ages 6 to 11, you should acquire skills that will prepare you to be a worker. These skills include learning to plan, making things, and using tools. The character virtue here is Industry. If you were successful in gaining this competence, you discovered pleasure in being productive and seeking success, and you developed a sense of competence. If you did not gain these competencies during this stage, it's possible that you developed a sense of inferiority and inadequacy.

Answer the questions about the memories you have related to this stage:

- What upsetting memories do I have during Stage 4?

- When I experience these memories, what thoughts come to mind?

- When I experience the thoughts related to these upsetting memories, what stories (Life Scripts) do I tell myself to make sense of these thoughts?

- What negative emotions do I feel when I tell myself these Life Scripts? Negative emotions can include feeling embarrassed, guilty, angry, outraged, sad, incompetent, afraid, anxious, hopeless, unhappy, nervous, disappointed, pessimistic, frustrated, regretful, lonely, inferior, panicky, and worthless.

Once again, to gain further insights into this stage of your life you may want to ask those who knew you during this time questions about your life, your parents, environment, and the events of significance that took place. In addition, you can also gain insights into your School Age experiences during this time by reading journals, looking at pictures of yourself, or watching home videos.

The information you receive from observers of your School Age stage may help you begin to unlock unconscious memories.

These memories may help you recall other memories from later stages of your life.

To gain some idea of whether or not Erikson's theory applies to you, answer the following existential question and then compare your answer with the other information you have collected about this stage of your development.

Generally speaking, do I think I can make it in the world of people and things?

Not at All   1...2...3...4...5...6...7...8...9...10   Absolutely

In keeping with the intent of this scale, I suggest that you seriously reflect on whether or not you are have confidence in your abilities. That is, if you have a sense of inferiority, often get frustrated when you fail at a task, and have little confidence in your ability to use personal skills to cope with the rigors of life, it's .quite possible that you did not successfully navigate this stage.

In light of the positive and negative outcomes explained in Columns 4 and 5 in Table 1d, I have provided you with some questions related to these outcomes as they correspond with this stage. These questions will help you gain insight into your own development and may also trigger memories or Life Scripts that have bearing on your present thoughts, emotions, attitudes, and actions. The questions are framed in a way that will help you think about whether or not you have experienced any number of positive or negative outcomes during this time in your life. The questions are as follows:

- Am I a competent person?

- Do I make things?

- Do I continue to learn and apply new skills?

- Do I have confidence in my ability to contribute?

- Do I pursue goals?

- Do I have the ability to apply myself?

- Do I find pleasure in being productive and being successful?

- Do I enjoy intellectual stimulation?

STAGE 4 INSIGHTS

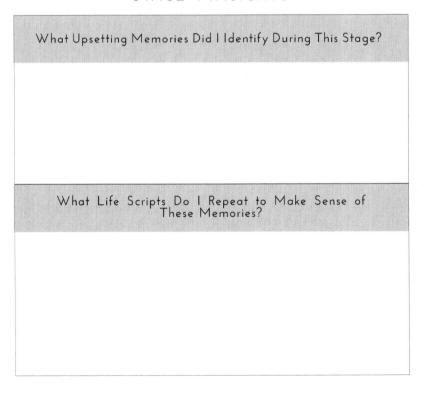

What Upsetting Memories Did I Identify During This Stage?

What Life Scripts Do I Repeat to Make Sense of These Memories?

STAGE 5: ADOLESCENCE

Ages 12 to 18 occur within the stage of Adolescence. During this crucial stage you question who you are, why you are here, where you came from, and where you are going. If you can answer these questions and successfully navigate this "identity crisis," you emerge from this fifth stage of development with a strong Identity. As a result, the character virtue you develop is Fidelity, or the ability to be true to yourself.

During this time, you should also begin to visualize a useful role and purpose in life. As a consequence of this vision of yourself as a unique and integrated person, you should also begin to develop increasing self- confidence and pride in your personal identity.

Table 1e

Summary of Erikson's Theory of Psychosocial Development

Approximate Age	Psycho-Social Crisis	Existential Question
Adolescence 12-18 years	Identity vs. Role Confusion	Who am I and what can I become?

Character Virtues & Positive Outcomes	Negative Outcomes (Arrested Development)
Fidelity evidenced by a coherent self-concept and a growing sense of personal identity and esteem, visualizing a useful role and purpose in life, self- confidence, personal standards and boundaries, social allegiance, discipline and discretion, pride, and personal identity. Seeing one's self as a unique and integrated person that has a role to play in the world, both in the present and the future.	**Confusion** over who and what one really is. Inability to identify a satisfactory or appropriate path or role in life. Uncertainty about how personal knowledge, skills, and abilities can be applied in a way that is meaningful in the present and/or the future. Lack of personal insight and appreciation for self and one's role in the world. No sense of having a legitimate place in the present or future. The belief that the world is conspiring against oneself.

If you experience arrested development at this stage you will, according to Erikson, experience a number of negative outcomes (see Column 5, Table 1e). These results can include confusion about who you are, what you stand for, your role in life, what you want to become, and your overall place in the world at large. You may also experience a lack of personal insight and appreciation for yourself.

Answer the questions about the memories you have related to this stage:

> • What upsetting memories do I have during Stage 5?

> • When I experience these memories, what thoughts come to mind?

> • When I experience the thoughts related to these upsetting memories, what stories do I tell myself to make sense of these thoughts?

> • What negative emotions do I feel when I tell myself these stories? Negative emotions can include feeling embarrassed, guilty, angry, outraged, sad, incompetent, afraid, anxious, hopeless, unhappy, nervous, disappointed, pessimistic, frustrated, regretful, lonely, inferior, panicky, and worthless.

To gain further insights into this stage of your life you may want to ask those who knew you during this time questions about what they observed about your life, your environment, and the events of significance that took place. In addition, you can gain insights into your adolescent experiences by looking at your secondary school yearbooks, reading journals, looking at pictures of yourself, or watching home videos.

As I have mentioned before, the information you receive from observers of your stage of Adolescence may help you begin to unlock unconscious memories. These memories may help you recall other memories and Life Scripts from later stages of your life.

To gain some idea of whether or not Erikson's theory applies to you, answer the following existential question and then compare your answer with the other information you have collected about this stage of your development.

Generally speaking, do I have a good sense of who I am, what I stand for, and what I can become?

Not at All   1...2...3...4...5...6...7...8...9...10   Absolutely

In consideration of the positive and negative outcomes explained in Columns 4 and 5 in Table 1e, I have provided you with some questions related to these outcomes as they correspond with your Adolescence. These questions will help you gain insight into your own development and may also trigger memories or Life Scripts that have bearing on your present thoughts, emotions, attitudes, and actions. The questions are framed in a way that will help you think about whether or not you have experienced any number of positive or negative outcomes during this time in your life. The questions are as follows:

• Do I have a good sense of personal identity and self-esteem?

• Do I have a clear vision of my role and purpose in life?

• Am I self-confident?

• Do I have clear personal standards and boundaries?

• Do I see myself as a unique and integrated person that has a role to play in the world, both in the present and the future?

STAGE 5 INSIGHTS

What Upsetting Memories Did I Identify During This Stage?
What Life Scripts Do I Repeat to Make Sense of These Memories?

STAGE 6: YOUNG ADULTHOOD

According to Erikson, no matter how successful you are in navigating previous stages and ultimately resolving your "identity crisis" in Stage 5, you are not developmentally complete until you are competent at Intimacy. Accordingly, ages 19 to 39 (Young Adulthood) represent the stage when you develop a competency of intimacy, which is required to prevent isolation. During this time you will think about your most important relationships as intimate, or Love, relationships.

Table 1f

Summary of Erikson's Theory of Psychosocial Development

Approximate Age	Psycho-Social Crisis	Existential Question
Young Adult 19-39 years	Intimacy vs. Isolation	Can I love?

Character Virtues & Positive Outcomes	Negative Outcomes (Arrested Development)
Love evidenced by the ability to give and receive love, developing and maintaining intimate emotional and physical connections with others, forming lasting reciprocating relationships and friendships, including positive relationships at work and in one's personal life. Ability to make and keep commitments to others.	**Inability to form affectionate relationships.** Fear of relationships with others. Feelings of isolation and aloneness. Fear of commitment. Difficulty making and sustaining long-term relationships with one or more individuals. Unable to depend on others.

As a healthy Young Adult, you should have the ability to give and receive love. You should also be able to develop and maintain intimate emotional and physical connections with others. This includes forming lasting reciprocating relationships at work and in your personal life. You should also develop the ability to make and keep commitments to others (see Column 4, Table 1f).

Arrested development during this stage of your life (see Column 5, Table 1f) may include negative outcomes like the inability to form affectionate relationships, fear of relationships, feelings of isolation and aloneness, and fear of commitment. Other signs of problems may include difficulty making and sustaining long-term relationships and/or retreating into isolation because you do not believe you can count on anyone other than yourself.

Answer the questions about the memories you have related to this stage:

- What upsetting memories do I have during Stage 6?

- When I experience these memories, what thoughts come to mind?

- When I experience the thoughts related to these upsetting memories, what stories do I tell myself to make sense of these thoughts?

- What negative emotions do I feel when I tell myself these stories? Negative emotions can include feeling embarrassed, guilty, angry, outraged, sad, incompetent, afraid, anxious, hopeless, unhappy, nervous, disappointed, pessimistic, frustrated, regretful, lonely, inferior, panicky, and worthless.

To gain further insights into this stage of your life ask those who knew you during this time questions regarding what they observed about your life, the environment, and the events of significance that took place. In addition, you can also gain insights into your Young Adult experiences by reading relevant newspapers or journals, looking at pictures of yourself, or watching home videos.

Once again, the information you receive from observers of your Young Adult stage may help you begin to unlock unconscious memories. These memories may help you recall other memories from later stages of your life.

To get some idea of whether or not Erikson's theory applies to you, answer the following existential question and then compare your answer with the other information you have collected about this stage of your development.

Generally speaking, can I love and make lasting commitments to others?

Not at All   1...2...3...4...5...6...7...8...9...10   Absolutely

You may also want to reflect on whether or not you are able to form affectionate relationships. If you tend to have difficulty making and sustaining long-term relationships with others, fear commitment, and/or frequently experience feelings of isolation and aloneness, it's possible that you did not successfully navigate this stage of your life.

In light of the positive and negative outcomes explained in Columns 4 and 5 in Table 1f, I have provided you with some questions related to these outcomes as they correspond with this stage. These questions will help you gain insight into your own development and may also trigger memories or Life Scripts that have bearing on your present thoughts, emotions, attitudes, and actions. The questions are framed in a way that will help you think about whether or not you have experienced any number of positive or negative outcomes during this time in your life. The questions are as follows:

- Do I have the ability to give and receive love?

- Have I been able to develop and maintain intimate emotional and physical connections with another person?

- Can I form lasting reciprocating relationships and friendships, including positive relationships at work and in my personal life?

- Do I have the ability to make and keep commitments to others?

STAGE 6 INSIGHTS

What Upsetting Memories Did I Identify During This Stage?

What Life Scripts Do I Repeat to Make Sense of
These Memories?

STAGE 7: MIDDLE ADULTHOOD

Ages 40 to 64 fall into the stage of Middle Adulthood. According to Erikson, during this seventh stage, healthy individuals begin to develop the trait of Generativity, which refers to the ability to look outside oneself and care for others, through parenting, mentoring, or voluntarily contributing to the larger community. Erikson illustrates this point by saying that "adults need children as much as children need adults" because of the developmental need we all have to learn to look outside ourselves.

Table 1g
Summary of Erikson's Theory of Psychosocial Development

Approximate Age	Psycho-Social Crisis	Existential Question
Middle Adult 40-64 years	Generativity vs. Stagnation	Can I make my life count?

Character Virtues & Positive Outcomes	Negative Outcomes (Arrested Development)
Caring as evidenced by unconditional love for children and family members, support and sacrifice for children, concern and voluntary service to others and the community, "thinking globally and acting locally," trying to make a difference in the world, building a legacy. Altruism demonstrated by an unselfish concern for the welfare of others, sacrificing to help others through a crisis or demanding situation or period in their life.	**Concerned only for self, one's own well-being, and prosperity.** Caught up in a self-centered lifestyle. A halt in personal growth or a sense of stagnation in life. No sense of contribution evidenced by trivializing one's activities. The inability to conceive oneself as a productive member of society.

A positive outcome of this stage is the attribute of Caring for others. You develop the desire and ability to help others, most specifically children, successfully navigate their own life stages (see Column 4, Table 1g). If you do not resolve this crisis, it's more likely that you will become self-centered and experience diminished personal growth (see Column 5, Table 1g).

Answer the questions about the memories you have related to this stage:

• What upsetting memories do I have during Stage 7?

• When I experience these memories, what thoughts come to mind?

• When I experience the thoughts related to these upsetting memories, what stories do I tell myself to make sense of these thoughts?

• What negative emotions do I feel when I tell myself these stories? Negative emotions can include feeling embarrassed, guilty, angry, outraged, sad, incompetent, afraid, anxious, hopeless, unhappy, nervous, disappointed, pessimistic, frustrated, regretful, lonely, inferior, panicky, and worthless.

To gain further insights into the Middle Adulthood stage of your life, you may want to ask those who knew you during this time questions about what they observed about your life, your environment, and the events of significance that took place. In addition, you can also gain insights into your Middle Adulthood experiences by reading journals or correspondence, looking at pictures of yourself, or watching home videos.

The information you receive from observers of this seventh stage may help you begin to unlock unconscious memories. These memories may help you recall other memories from later stages of your life.

To get some idea of whether or not Erikson's theory applies to you, answer the following existential question and then compare your answer with the other information you have collected about this stage of your development.

Generally speaking, have I been able to make my life count?

Not at All   1...2...3...4...5...6...7...8...9...10   Absolutely

If you scored low on this scale, it's possible that you have not successfully navigated the psychosocial crisis during this stage of your life. For example, if you are caught up in a self-centered lifestyle, mostly focussed on your own wellbeing, and/or sense that you are no longer growing as a person, it's quite possible that the stories you tell yourself to make sense of this life stage are irrational. Accordingly, I suggest that you examine these stories carefully to determine whether or not they are rational.

Finally, given the positive and negative outcomes explained in Columns 4 and 5 in Table 1g, I have provided you with some questions related to these outcomes as they correspond with this stage. These questions will help you gain insight into your own development and may also trigger memories or Life Scripts that have bearing on your present thoughts, emotions, attitudes, and actions. The questions are framed in a way that will help you think about whether or not you have experienced a positive or negative outcome related to the constructs discussed under this stage of development. The questions are as follows:

• Do I care about and have unconditional love for children and family members?

• Do I support and sacrifice for children?

• Do I have concern for and provide voluntary service to others and the community?

• Do I try to make a difference in the world?

• Am I trying to build a personal legacy?

• Do I have an unselfish concern for the welfare of others as evidenced by a willingness to sacrifice to help others through a crisis or demanding situation in their life?

STAGE 7 INSIGHTS

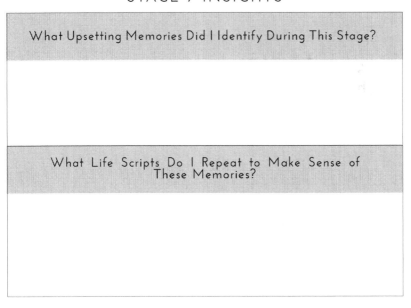

What Upsetting Memories Did I Identify During This Stage?

What Life Scripts Do I Repeat to Make Sense of These Memories?

STAGE 8: OLDER ADULT

The ages of 65 until death (Older Adult) provide the time for individuals to reflect upon their lives and their contribution in the grand scheme of things. It's a time when you think of your life as being filled with pleasure and satisfaction or with disappointments and failure.

Table 1h
Summary of Erikson's Theory of Psychosocial Development

Approximate Age	Psycho-Social Crisis	Existential Question
Older Adult 65-death	Ego Integrity vs. Despair	Is it okay to have been me?

Character Virtues & Positive Outcomes	Negative Outcomes (Arrested Development)
Wisdom as evidenced by serenity, tolerance, reconciling regrets, accepting the inevitability of physical decline and death, imparting life lessons to posterity, peace of mind, spiritual reflection, and reconciliation, accepting loss and the departure of friends and family. A sense of integrity and fulfillment, and a willingness to face death.	**Dissatisfaction with life.** A sense of despair. Many regrets about the past and lost opportunities. Refusal to consider having made a meaningful contribution in the past. Lack of hope. Consumed with a sense of bitterness and despair regarding the future. A fear of death.

According to Erikson, when you reach the Older Adult stage, you begin to compare what you have done across your life span against your sense of what you should have done. If the results of your analysis are positive, you will likely be satisfied and fulfilled in a way that you can accept death with a sense of accomplishment and Ego Integrity. If, on the other hand, you believe you have fallen short of your potential and you do not look at your life and accomplishments as particularly meaningful, you will likely despair and fear death. The positive attribute that is developed during this final stage of development is Wisdom.

Answer the questions about the memories you have related to this stage:

• What upsetting memories do I have during Stage 8?

• When I experience these memories, what thoughts come to mind?

• When I experience the thoughts related to these upsetting memories, what stories do I tell myself to make sense of these thoughts?

• What negative emotions do I feel when I tell myself these stories? Negative emotions can include feeling embarrassed, guilty, angry, outraged, sad, incompetent, afraid, anxious, hopeless, unhappy, nervous, disappointed, pessimistic, frustrated, regretful, lonely, inferior, panicky, and worthless.

To get some idea of whether or not Erikson's theory applies to you, answer the following existential question and then compare your answer with the other information you have collected about this stage of your development.

Generally speaking, do I believe it is okay to have been me?

Not at All   1...2...3...4...5...6...7...8...9...10   Absolutely

Finally, considering the positive and negative outcomes explained in Columns 4 and 5 in Table 1h, I have provided you with some questions related to these outcomes as they correspond with this stage. These questions will help you gain insight into your own development and may also trigger memories or Life Scripts that have bearing on your present thoughts, emotions, attitudes, and actions. The questions are framed in a way that will help you think about whether or not you have experienced a positive or negative outcome related to this final stage of development. The questions are as follows:

- Do I think of myself as a wise person?

- Do I attempt to impart wisdom to others about what I have learned in life?

- Do I have a sense of serenity and peace when I think about where I am in life and my life as a whole?

- Have I been able to reconcile regrets in my life?

- Am I able to accept loss and the departure of my friends and family?

- Am I willing to face my ultimate decline and death with courage and peace?

STAGE 8 INSIGHTS

What Upsetting Memories Did I Identify During This Stage?

What Life Scripts Do I Repeat to Make Sense of These Memories?

CONSIDERING HOW IRRATIONAL BELIEFS MAY CONTRIBUTE TO IRRATIONAL LIFE SCRIPTS

Albert Ellis, in his Rational Emotive Behavior Therapy (REBT), identified a number of dysfunctional beliefs that people often hold that, in this context, may serve as markers of irrational Life Scripts. Ellis lists eleven specific examples of irrational beliefs that tend to spawn irrational thinking:

1) It is a dire necessity for me to be loved or approved by almost all others who are significant to me;

2) I must be thoroughly competent, adequate, and achieving in all important respects in order to be worthwhile;

3) The world must be fair. People must act fairly and considerately, and if they do not, they are bad, wicked, villainous, or incredibly stupid; they should be severely blamed and punished;

4) It is awful and terrible when things are not the way I very much want them to be;

5) There is not much I can do about my anxiety, anger, depression, or unhappiness because my feelings are caused by what happens to me;

6) If something is dangerous or dreadful, I should be constantly and excessively upset about it and should dwell on the possibility of it occurring;

7) It is easier to avoid and to put off facing life's difficulties and responsibilities than face them;

8) I'm quite dependent on others and need someone stronger than myself to rely upon; I can't run my own life;

9) My past history mainly causes my present feelings and behavior; things from my past, which once strongly influenced me, will always strongly influence me;

10) I must become very anxious, angry, or depressed over someone else's problems and disturbances if I care about that person; and

11) There is a right and perfect solution to almost all problems, and it is awful not to find it.

In view of these irrational beliefs and the purpose of this ACT (which is to identify irrational Life Scripts), I suggest that you carefully consider each irrational belief. Then compare them against your own beliefs, thoughts, and stories as a way to identify any irrational Life Scripts.

More specifically, as you consider each of the eleven irrational beliefs ask yourself, "Do I hold this belief?" If you answer yes, ask yourself: 1) what upsetting thoughts do I think as a consequence of holding this belief, 2) what stories do I tell myself to make sense of this belief, and 3) what negative impact does thinking these thoughts and telling myself these stories have on my life? If indeed, you do determine that you tell yourself upsetting stories as a consequence of holding one or more of these beliefs, please include these stories in your list of irrational Life Scripts.

INSIGHTS RELATED TO IRRATIONAL BELIEFS

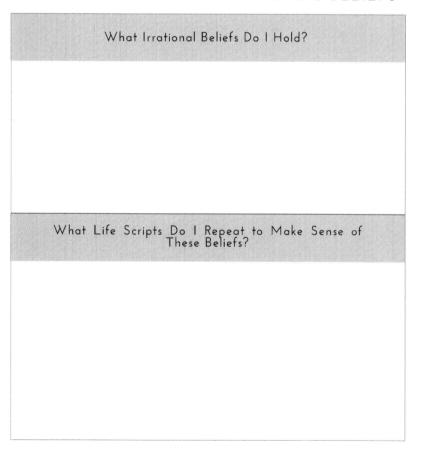

What Irrational Beliefs Do I Hold?

What Life Scripts Do I Repeat to Make Sense of These Beliefs?

ONE FINAL SWEEP TO PICK UP IRRATIONAL SCRIPTS YOU MAY HAVE MISSED

In addition to answering the questions related to Erikson's psychosocial stages, it's also helpful to think about some very practical considerations when trying to identify irrational Life Scripts. First, think about the different roles you have played and now play in your life, including the different relationships you have with family, friends, supervisors, religious leaders, partners, clients, and so on. As you think about these roles, ask yourself what you have thought, said, or done in these roles that has been ineffective. That is, try to recall upsetting memories during times when 1) your intended communication was consistently misunderstood by the person(s) you were trying to reach and influence; 2) your communication with someone may have been broken in some way and does not continue; 3) you do or did try to reach out and communicate to bring some resolution to the disagreements that have caused a broken relationship, and your attempts at communication caused even more discomfort or misunderstanding; and/or 4) what you have needed to do did not get done or may have consistently been done incorrectly. This process will help you recognize circular patterns you may have found yourself that you continue to experience as they relate to relationships and roles you played and/or are currently playing. You may recognize these maladaptive patterns in the definition of insanity, which is "doing the same thing over and over again and expecting a different result."

Based on your reflections regarding your ineffective transactions with others in the various roles you have played, taken together with your circular patterns of personal "insanity," list the upsetting memories you recall. Also write out the irrational Life Scripts you have repeated to make sense of these memories.

OTHER INSIGHTS

What Other Upsetting Memories Do I Recall?
What Life Scripts Do I Repeat to Make Sense of These Memories?

ACT III

RESTRUCTURING IRRATIONAL LIFE SCRIPTS: THE PATH TO A BRAND NEW YOU

In 2013, Jason Headley released a short on YouTube entitled, "It's Not About the Nail" (http://www.youtube.com/watch?v=-4EDhdAHrOg). Headley's short video is a powerful way of portraying individuals who incessantly want other people to listen to their problems as a means of getting some kind of cathartic relief without seeking a solution. In this situation, this individual will always come up disappointed, no matter how good the listener is, because he or she is ignoring the root cause of the problem. That is, if you have a proverbial nail in your head, you must "get it out" before you can get permanent relief. This is also true with irrational Life Scripts (stories that are not true, do not help us solve our problems and/or achieve our goals) that we tell ourselves to make sense of any part of our life experience. Any story you repeat in your head that is not going to help you get what you want in your life must be "taken out" before you can start moving in a direction of recovery.

For example, I once had an obese client who wanted me to help him lose a significant amount of weight. I began to listen to the stories he had told himself over time to justify eating into a state of obesity. After listening during the first few minutes of our session, I said, "I've got it! You tell yourself that you must eat whatever you want in order to be happy." He replied, "Yes. And why not?"

I then asked, "Do you eat whatever you want?" He said, "Yes." I followed with another simply question, "Are you happy?" I could almost see the lightbulb flash in his head when he said, "No." He then said something like "Wow, that sounds crazy! I have been telling myself a lie and I didn't realize it until this moment!"

This example illustrates the point that you must pull the irrational stories you tell yourself out of your head (get the nail out) before you can start moving forward. And sometimes, in the case of my overweight client, it may be useful during this process to seek out the help of a professional.

ACT III will further illustrate why simply finding someone to listen to your troubles and insisting that they listen until you "get it all out" will not help resolve your emotional pain if you have a nail (irrational story) in your head. It will also explain what you must do to pull out the nail because frankly in some instances, "it is all about the nail."

There are two parts to ACT III. The first is to write new, rational Life Scripts to replace the irrational ones identified in ACT II. This is diagrammatically illustrated in Figure 1. After studying Figure 1, consider new, rational stories you should tell yourself instead of the irrational stories you have relied on in the past.

Figure 1
The Life Script Restructuring Process

Irrational Life Scripts (Stories I Tell Myself That Upset Me and Cause Me to Think and Act Irrationally)	Rational Life Scripts (New Stories I Plan To Tell Myself INSTEAD OF the Old Stories)

*When something bad happens, you have three choices:
You can either let it define you. Let it destroy you. Or
you can let it strengthen you. - Unknown*

Part 2 of this ACT is to evaluate the rationality of the new scripts and determine your readiness to play the parts dictated in each script. In this part you will consider a number of questions that relate to rational criteria and assess your readiness to change by adopting the new Life Scripts.

ACT III, PART 1
THE WHATS AND HOWS OF
WRITING NEW LIFE SCRIPTS

A basic principle of Life Script Restructuring is that you are responsible for your own behavior. The environment, your early childhood, the effects of your culture, and the way you were socialized have played a significant role in your development. Nevertheless, LSR assumes you are capable of making decisions that enable you to overcome and move beyond counterproductive and destructive internal stories resulting from your past experiences. It assumes that you can change and become the kind of person you want to be, regardless of your past experience and decisions. This is done by rewriting, and thereby restructuring, your Life Scripts in a way that creates healthier, more constructive internal dialogues for directing your everyday thoughts and actions.

This is the point in the LSR process where you have the opportunity to restructure the irrational Life Scripts you identified in ACT II. By restructure, I mean edit or completely rewrite the old scripts in a way that ensures the new scripts are rational and effective in helping re-direct and re-engineer how you see yourself and your future. If done correctly, this process will help you systematically manufacture a life that is exciting and fulfilling simply by writing and following your new Life

Scripts. Truly devoting yourself to this process will cause you to soon be able to discern both fundamental and permanent change in your very nature.

The LSR process makes this change possible by leveraging brain plasticity so that you can see yourself in a way that allows you to do what is required to become the kind of person who can do the kinds of things you want to do in life (Cole, 2013). Once you create and embrace rational Life Scripts that are based on the kind of life you want to live, you will naturally conform to these scripts and reject anything that is incongruent with this new way of being.

There are many ways to write a Life Script. The important thing is to write your script in a way that works for you.

> Everyone has a story, make your own worth telling.
> - Patrick Rickets

This first step is to make a list of all the irrational Life Scripts you identified in ACT II. Secondly, rank these scripts from most to least important in terms of which ones you want to change. The "most important" irrational Life Script is the one that is causing you the most trouble. Conversely, the least important is the script that is causing you trouble, but not enough to worry about at the moment.

Once you have decided on the irrational script you want to tackle first, begin the process of writing the new Life Script. This process will be the same for each script and includes the following steps:

1) Brainstorm, conduct research, and talk to others about ideas for new scripts. This process will help you get some fresh ideas and perspectives that can help you see the old script differently while, at the same time, help you generate ideas for new scripts.

If you are having difficulty coming up with ideas for a new script, you may want to schedule time with a therapist or life coach. These professionals are trained to help you clarify your problems and see solutions that you may not have considered. This process is illustrated in the last section of this book (the Postscript) where I provide some examples of how I have helped my clients transform their old stories into new, rational Life Scripts.

2) Formulate a premise that is a short phrase or sentence that gets at the heart of what you want to think and do when you play the new part. This is the core idea or message behind your new script. For example, if you have identified an irrational Life Script that has caused you to play a "self-centered" role in life, you could write a new, rational Life Script that is based on the premise that states "I am anxiously engaged in good causes."

3) The next step is to create an outline of the script. This is a basic plan that you will use to direct your thoughts and actions toward playing the new role. The outline must be succinct and specific so that you have a clear vision of how events will unfold as you become the character in the script. For example, in keeping with the example I provided in step 2, if you plan to move away from living a self-centered life with a new script that has the premise, "I am anxiously engaged in good causes," your outline could include points like: 1) What constitutes a good cause, 2) The problems associated with being self-centered, 3) The benefits of assisting in "good causes," and/or 4) The amount of time and effort I will contribute to good causes each month.

4) Flesh out your new story under each point in your outline. The following questions will help you think about the specifics you should include in your new story. As you answer each question, you will begin to see what you need to do differently (more or less of) to overcome the problems caused by the irrational Life Script you are editing or replacing with this new Script. The questions will also help ensure that your new Life Script is both realistic, complete, and effective.

- What do I need to think more about to overcome my irrational Life Script?

- What do I need to think less about to overcome my irrational Life Script?

- What do I need to do more of to overcome my irrational Life Script?

- What do I need to do less of to overcome my irrational Life Script?

- Where do I need to spend more time to overcome my irrational Life Script?

- Where do I need to spend less time to overcome my irrational Life Script?

- With whom should I spend more time to overcome my irrational Life Script?

> • With whom should I spend less time to overcome my irrational Life Script?

> • What will prevent me from thinking and doing the things required to overcome my irrational Life Script?

In addition to considering these questions, it's also helpful to think about the different roles you have played in your irrational Life Scripts in the different relationships you have with family, friends, supervisors, religious leaders, partners, clients, and so on. As you think about these roles you played, you can decide what you need to think or do differently to leave these roles and take on new ones.

Some of the irrational roles people tend to play in irrational Life Scripts can include being a victim, judge, self-righteous onlooker, nurturer, enabler, savior, perpetrator, and so on. These are just a few of the roles you may have played in the scripts you identified in ACT II. In order to change these roles, you must write a script with a role that is rational and that helps you become the kind of person you want to be and live the kind of life you want to live.

If you keep telling the same sad small story, you will keep living the same sad small life. - Jean Houston

As you first go through the process of filling in the details of your new story, keep it simple and straightforward. Because you are playing the part in the story you are writing, you will not need too much detail to know what you are talking about. Do not worry about style, format, or anything else that gets in the way of reminding yourself of what you want to think, say, and do as you play out the part you are writing for yourself.

5) Go through your script and simplify the new story. Make it as "user friendly" as possible. Only keep the detail you need to remind yourself of what you will do to play your part. Provide yourself a sense of what's going to happen as you play the new part.

As you trim down your story, look for dead weight, weak links, irrelevant details, over-explaining, sidetracking, elements that drag, and anything else that weakens the overall trajectory. Be harsh; just because you fell in love with something you wrote in the exploratory phase doesn't mean it should survive the revision phase.

6) Since the new script requires you to think, say, and do different things than you did in your irrational script, spend a lot of time working on specific thoughts you will think and actions you will take INSTEAD OF the things you thought and did in your previous irrational role. This strategy is extremely important in the early stages of your new role.

7) Show your finished work to someone you know and trust. Ask for opinion and input. Choose people who are trustworthy and also willing to provide honest feedback. Their feedback will help you think about things you have not considered.

8) Revise your new Life Script based on the feedback you get in Step 7. In fact, revise your work as many times as necessary. Painful as it may be, you will be glad when you are finally able to convey your vision.

ACT III, PART 2
EVALUATING YOUR NEW LIFE SCRIPTS
FOR RATIONALITY AND EFFECTIVENESS

The first step in evaluating your new Life Scripts for rationality is to ask yourself whether or not the new stories meet the rational criteria introduced earlier in the book. If they do, then it's more likely that the scripts are rational. Once again, to be rational, your life scripts about who you are and the role you "should" play in your world must 1) help you develop and sustain a rational self-identity; 2) be logical and consistent with known facts and reality—based on truth; 3) produce desired emotions;

> Our plans miscarry because they have no aim. When a man does not know what harbor he is making for, no wind is the right wind. - Seneca

4) help overcome current and future problems; 5) encourage serenity, personal growth, development, and happiness; 6) encourage learning from the past, preparing for the future, and living in the present; 7) support personal and interpersonal goals; and 8) support an optimistic view of one's self and future. If, on the other hand, your life scripts 1) cause you to form an irrational sense of self identity; 2) are not logical and/or there is no evidence to support their truth; 3) do not help you feel

the way you want to feel; 4) do not help you overcome your problems; 5) are destructive to yourself or others; and/or 6) undermines your goals and your ability to become your highest and best self, they are irrational and will cause you any number of problems until they are either edited or rewritten completely into cohesive Life Scripts that support a rational, healthy life.

In addition to meeting the rational criteria, you must be committed to play the new role outlined in each script. If you are not committed, the script may be beautifully written and explicated in a way that will help you experience what you want in life, but will be completely useless because you will not follow it. To help you sort out this conflict, I suggest that you answer the following questions as they relate to each of your new Life Scripts. I have framed these questions as if I were answering them to provide a pattern for you to follow.

1) Am I commited to this script? If I'm not, I need to rewrite the script until the likelihood that I will live by it is in the 90% range. After all, why should I try to live by a script that I am not committed to?

2) What do I plan to accomplish by living this script? If I have a clear idea about what I am trying to accomplish, I will have a much better idea as to whether or not I can do what it takes to follow the new script. If I do not have a precise understanding of where I am going and what I am going to do, I probably won't get there.

3) What will I need to do to prepare to live by this new script? Getting prepared before launching into this new role is crucial.

This preparation should include making a plan of action and visualizing how I will succeed before I begin the hard work of succeeding.

4) When will I start living by this new script? Setting a start date is exciting for me. For example, if I plan to start a new exercise program I need to spend some time deciding on the type of exercises I will engage in, as well as when, where, and how often I will perform these activities.

5) What barriers may I encounter when trying to live by this new Life Script? Answering this question will help me anticipate the people, places, or things that may prevent me from playing my new role. This information helps me plan what I will need to think and/or do differently to overcome barriers to successfully live by what is outlined in the script.

6) How will I know if I succeed and follow the new role that I have outlined for myself? If I can see the outcome of my new role and it's a good one, I am motivated by this vision of my success. In the case of writing this book, I could see the book being advertised and sold on Amazon. I could see many people benefiting from the principles of Life Script Restructuring. And, I could see my work becoming more efficient and effective with my clients and students as they readily refer to these principles in session and in the classroom.

The second of the six questions I had asked myself is, "What do I plan to accomplish?" This question relates to the many elements that make up a Life Script, including directives for what you want to BE, KNOW, DO, FEEL, and ACQUIRE. For example, you can direct yourself to 1) BE more confident, self-disciplined, patient, trustworthy, or assertive; 2) KNOW or learn more about your spouse, automobiles, a profession, or cooking; 3) DO something, like finishing a gardening project, losing weight, or exercising four times per week; 4) FEEL differently (less angry or more committed) about someone or something, like your job, your spouse, your living circumstances, or a wayward child; and/or 5) ACQUIRE something you want that you do not currently have, like a new car, a home, an honor at work, a big screen television, a boat, or a degree.

As a reminder, the new Life Scripts you have written are designed to help you become someone different than you currently are by helping you re-direct and re-engineer how you see yourself and your future. The reasoning behind this idea is that you simply cannot do certain things in life unless you become the kind of person who does those kinds of things.

Finally, to make absolutely certain that your new Life Scripts are what they need to be to cause the change toward becoming the person you want to become, do one final assessment by asking yourself the following questions. (You may want to compare your answers with the ones you gave in Act I about goal setting.):

- Do I truly believe I can play the role outlined in this script?

- Do I have what it takes to play this part (e.g., knowledge, skills, resources, support)?

• Based on my responses to the last question, what do I need to think or do to play the new role?

How committed am I to playing this new part? (circle number)

(no commitment) 0 -- 1 -- 2 -- 3 -- 4 -- 5 -- 6 -- 7 -- 8 -- 9 --10 (totally committed)

How confident am I that I can play this part? (circle number)

(no confidence) 0 -- 1 -- 2 -- 3 -- 4 -- 5 -- 6 -- 7 -- 8 -- 9 --10 (totally confident)

How prepared am I? (circle number)

(no preparation) 0 -- 1 -- 2 -- 3 -- 4 -- 5 -- 6 -- 7 -- 8 -- 9 --10 (totally prepared)

• What do I need to raise each number I circled to a 10?

• What else do I need to follow the script? Improved self-image, knowledge, skills, social support, money?

After you have written and evaluated the first Life Script that will replace your most problematic irrational Life Script, repeat the process with all the irrational scripts you plan to restructure. You will notice that many of the irrational scripts you identified in ACT II will be addressed by the first new Life Script you write. This is because irrational stories tend to "run in packs," so to speak. Core beliefs, thoughts, and actions that make up your most pressing irrational scripts tend to impact all of your maladaptive scripts. Because of this, you will only need to write a few new scripts to get at the root causes of your upsetting stories. This efficiency is most noticeable if you are conscientious and thorough with the first few rational Life Scripts you write.

The final ACT directs you to learn, to use, and then apply a number of techniques that will help you internalize and maintain your new lifestyle as dictated by your new scripts. These techniques include mental imagery, self hypnosis, and mental monitoring activities that will help instill deep in your subconscious the new thoughts and actions that are prescribed in your new, rational Life Scripts.

ACT IV

MENTALLY PROGRAMMING, INTERNALIZING, AND MAINTAINING YOUR NEW LIFE SCRIPTS

Now that you have identified your irrational Life Scripts and restructured and replaced them with new, rational Life Scripts, it's time to set these new scripts deep into your psyche so that they become your mental "path of least resistance" as you consciously and unconsciously think and act out your life. You can do this by using techniques designed to leverage your brain's neuroplasticity.

Neuroplasticity is the brain's ability to be flexible and change in function and structure. It starts before you are born and continues throughout your life.

There are two primary causes of brain adaptation. These are environmental exposures (experience-dependent neuroplasticity) and self-directed attention (self-directed neuroplasticity).

Experience-dependent neuroplasticity occurs when you interact with the environment. Because it's an unconscious process of brain adaptation, it's considered to be "automatic."

Your beliefs become your
thoughts,
Your thoughts become your
words,
Your words become your actions,
Your actions become your habits,
Your habits become your values,

Self-directed neuroplasticity is the conscious process described in this ACT. It involves using mental imagery techniques to direct your attention in a way that physically sculpts, trains, and conditions your brain. These techniques include meditation, visualization, mental imagery, and hypnosis. Because of brain plasticity, you can purposefully direct your attention in a way that enables you to rewire your brain, after sufficient repetition, in a way that helps you permanently change your Life Scripts.

Given all the evidence that self-directed attention activities can change neural pathways, I recommend that you attempt to document these changes as they occur. When working with my clients in clinical settings, I ask them to do this by looking for a "Flash of Ideas." This "flash" usually occurs within four to six days after they begin using a self-directed attention activity to change a Life Script. I base this suggestion on the fact that, according to neuroscience researchers, observable changes can be seen in neural pathways within a matter of days (Hanson, Mendius, 2009).

Typically, clients are anxious to look for the "Flash of Ideas." When they complete the assigned self-directed attention activity with sufficient intensity, they often do report some type of "enlightenment" or "epiphany-like" experience. Because of this consistently reported outcome, I now tell my clients to record everything that comes to them and report back to me the highlights of their experience. Some of these highlights include statements like the following:

"I experienced an enlightened understanding!"

"I had a breakthrough on my dieting. I will never be overweight again."

"When the therapeutic methodology clicked, it was like seeing and drinking a glass of pure hope! It was like being hot and sweaty and seeing a cold glass of water that tastes better than it looks!"

"It was like my mind expanded and I could finally see what you were talking about in our last session!"

"I had a sudden stroke of ideas that helped me overcome a problem I have struggled with for years!"

"I had this very strong desire to improve myself and others."

"I experienced a surge of motivation!"

"My heart was filled with love for myself and my wife!"

"The goals have helped me create a path that has caused me to meet like-minded people."

"I can see it!"

Given this remarkable feedback, I recommend that you also look for a "Flash of Ideas" when you are using the self-directed attention exercises described in this ACT. When you experience this type of enlightenment, write it down—then savor and ponder the impressions. These impressions and ideas can be effectively used to permanently change your Life Scripts.

We are what we repeatedly do. Excellence, then, is not an act, but a habit. - Aristotle

ACT IV in the LSR process provides you with a number of straightforward techniques that will systematically leverage your brain plasticity in a way that mentally programs and helps you internalize and maintain your new, rational Life Scripts. These techniques are described in two parts.

Part 1 includes mental imagery and self-hypnosis techniques that you will use to rehearse your new Life Scripts. Part 2 is a mental monitoring technique that explains how to maintain your new Life Scripts as you inevitably deal with change and the challenges of life.

ACT IV, PART 1

Part 1 of ACT IV involves using your imagination to program your mind and internalize your new Life Scripts. To use your imagination effectively, you must first realize it takes enormous power to visualize objects, situations, circumstances, responses to impulses, sound, taste, and other sensations. The capacity to imagine is built into every person and is activated at a very young age. It is the ability to think about people, places, and things beyond your present situation. It is a fundamental aspect of the human condition that allows us to transcend our present circumstances and think about the future, remember the past, solve problems in the present, and strategize about how to effectively create and implement new ideas and Life Scripts.

Self-Hypnosis, Visualization, Mental Imaging, and Rehearsal are synthetic learning techniques that rely on your creative imagination to help you improve the rationality and congruence between your thoughts, Life Scripts, and actions. Part 1 of this ACT guides you in how to use these techniques to increase your commitment and intensity toward consistently playing the new role you have outlined for yourself in your new, rational Life Scripts.

When using these techniques, you can increase your internal motivation and intensity toward playing your new roles with things like motivational literature, pictures, images, videos, and music that are in sync with what you are trying to accomplish. For example, by mentally creating, recreating, and focusing on the parts you have decided to play, and then anticipating and focusing on ways of overcoming barriers to this role, you can acquire and amplify the personal confidence required to make your new Life Scripts a reality.

The visualization and imagery techniques I recommend are applied across four steps. These include: 1) writing rational Life Scripts (completed in ACT III), 2) creating a place in your mind for doing your mental work, 3) learning to relax, and 4) using the mental exercises to rehearse, mentally program, and internalize your new scripts.

Step 1: Writing New Life Scripts

You have already created new Life Scripts in ACT III. At this point, begin to decide on which scripts and which parts of the script you want to practice in your mental imagery session. This should be carefully laid out in your mind before going to the place where you will do the mental work.

Step 2: Constructing Places in Your Mind

It's important to construct a "place in your mind" when you are doing your visualization and imagery work. The mental place I recommend that everyone learn to use in Life Script Restructuring exercises is called a "Mental Home Movie Theater." This is because it's easy for anyone who has watched television or a movie to visualize and apply in this context.

Begin by creating a movie theater in your mind, including seating and a screen. This is where you will watch yourself play out your parts in the new scripts you created in ACT III.

Step 3: Relaxing Before Using Mental Imagery

It's important that you learn how to relax when using any type of visualization, mental imagery, or self-hypnosis technique. To help you with this I have provided you with both Deep Breathing (3a) and Progressive Muscle Relaxation Techniques (3b). Taken together or used separately, these techniques will help you learn to relax in a way that improves your ability to focus and attend to your self-directed visualization and imagery assignments.

The steps you should follow when using the Deep Breathing and/ or the Progressive Muscle Relaxation techniques are outlined below. Once again, the purpose of these relaxation techniques is to help you prepare for the visualization and imagery exercises that follow.

3a: The Deep Breathing Exercise

Get in a comfortable position.

Close your eyes.

Breathe in through your nose and out through your mouth. As you breathe in through your nose, visualize inhaling pure oxygen that is coated with relaxation.

As you breathe out through your mouth, exaggerate the exhalation by visualizing blowing out a birthday candle and imagining that you are releasing tension, stress, and strain. The exaggerated exhalation will speed up the relaxation process.

Continue breathing in and out until you are able to feel a sense of calm and have quieted most of the distracting thoughts (e.g., your internal critic) that may interfere with your imagery exercise.

You can now use the Progressive Muscle Relaxation technique or, if you feel relaxed, go ahead and start the visualization and imagery exercise.

3b: The Progressive Muscle Relaxation

Find a comfortable position.

Close your eyes.

Visualize scanning your body up and down to find an area that is "more" relaxed than most other places on your body.

See yourself breathing into that area (in through your nose and out through your mouth) while imagining that your inhalation is causing the "more" relaxed area to increase in diameter and your exhalation is releasing stress.

Do this for about 30 seconds.

Now visualize yourself scanning your body to find an area that is more tense than the other parts of your body. Once you have identified this area, start breathing in and out. Once again, imagine that your inhalation is relaxing the area that is "more" tense than other areas in your body. Do this for about 30 seconds.

Now start tensing and relaxing muscle groups from your feet to your head while breathing in pure oxygen/relaxation and breathing out stress/tension/strain.

Imagine flexing the muscles in your feet for 5 seconds and then releasing. The tensing of muscles will bring blood to the area where you have flexed and will cause a sense of warmth and relaxation. Continue breathing in and out while continuing to imagine taking in pure oxygen and releasing stress and strain.

Now flex your lower legs for 5 seconds, your calf muscles, while repeating the breathing process.

Next, go to your upper legs, then buttocks, abdomen, chest and back, hands, arms, shoulders, neck, and then face. Flex each muscle area for 5 seconds and then release while continuing to breathe throughout the entire process. Continue to focus on breathing in pure oxygen and exhaling all the bad things that are causing your body to tense up and feel stress.

After go through the muscle groups, you should be prepared to start the imagery exercise. If not, go through the process of tensing and relaxing your muscles again and again until you are feeling calm.

Begin the visualization and imagery exercise.

Step 4: The Visualization and Imagery Exercise

Now that you have relaxed you can begin using the visualization and imagery exercises to rehearse and internalize your new scripts. There are several steps you can follow to increase your abilities in these mental processes:

Decide which Life Scripts or parts of these scripts you plan to work on during this rehearsal session. Also, decide what your goals are as you rehearse. For example, "I plan to mentally rehearse all of my Life Scripts about how I relate to my spouse," or, "I will rehearse my Life Script that directs how I will resist pressure to use alcohol and other drugs."

After deciding on your assignment, you will start the process at a conscious baseline, which is the mental state of awareness that you live in when you go about your day-to-day activities.

Tune inward with the initial focus on a slow relaxed breath, while at the same time imagining that you are going into a deeper state while counting down slowly from 5, 4, 3, 2, to 1.

After getting relaxed, close your eyes and go to the "Mental Home Movie Theater" in your mind.

Use your imagination to watch yourself pull out the script(s) you plan to work on during this "practice session."

At this point, use all of your senses to work on the scripts you have assigned yourself to work on.

Focus on the present as if you are the character that you are watching on screen.

Watch yourself play your part in the mental movie over and over again until you believe you are the character you are watching.

When making suggestions use "I am" instead of "I will be" statements. For example, "I am relaxed when I give my speech," or "I am responding to an angry customer in a relaxed, calm, effective manner," or "I am running every morning before breakfast," or "I am only eating foods that keep me healthy and strong!"

Visualize yourself rehearsing until you achieve a perfect performance and have the confidence that you can effectively play the part you have rehearsed.

End your exercise with affirmations that will bring positive benefits from this experience. For example, "I am gaining great confidence in my ability to play this new role," or "I can see myself improving in this area of my life," or "This rehearsal has helped me improve my ability to act out my part in this new, rational Life Script!"

You are going to become alert and come out of this deeply relaxed state after counting to three: 1, 2, and 3.

Return to your conscious baseline.

Record your progress in your journal so you can carry your accomplishments and good memories with you.

ACT IV: PART 2

Part 2 in ACT IV will help you learn to systematically observe and master your thoughts and internal monologues—the stories you tell yourself to make sense of your thoughts—to ensure that they are consistent with, and supportive of, your new Life Scripts. You will do this by learning to observe your thoughts, evaluate them against your new Life Scripts, discard those thoughts that do not support and are not aligned with your new scripts, and replace irrational thoughts with thoughts and stories that are supportive of your new Life Scripts.

This process is illustrated in Figure 2a, the "Thoughts, Emotions, (Re)Actions Diagram," which illustrates how Life Script Restructuring works. As you can see in this figure, we all have thoughts that influence how we feel—namely, our emotions. The logic illustrated here is that if you think or tell yourself stories that are irrational, you will feel upset and, in turn, act irrationally (Re-Act) unless you somehow filter out irrational thoughts and stories.

Figure 2a

The Thoughts, Emotions, (Re)Actions Diagram

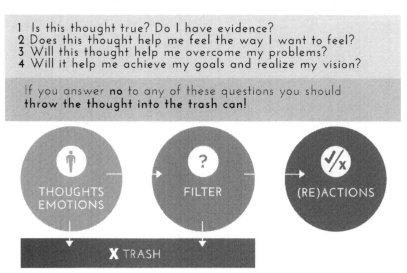

1 Is this thought true? Do I have evidence?
2 Does this thought help me feel the way I want to feel?
3 Will this thought help me overcome my problems?
4 Will it help me achieve my goals and realize my vision?

If you answer **no** to any of these questions you should **throw the thought into the trash can!**

THOUGHTS EMOTIONS → FILTER ? → (RE)ACTIONS

X TRASH

To overcome this maladaptive process, you can place filters, in the form of rational questions, in your thought process. These questions are designed to help you filter out irrational thoughts.

Once the questions you have chosen to filter out irrational thoughts are in place (your Rational Mental Filters), you will use them to help you examine your thoughts and stories and "throw out" the ones that are irrational and/or inconsistent with your new Life Scripts.

Once again, each of the Rational Mental Filters in Figure 2a is a different question that you will ask of your thoughts in an effort to distinguish the rational ones from the irrational ones. Simply put, when you learn to pay careful attention to your thoughts, you will begin to ask yourself whether or not the thoughts you are entertaining, and the stories you tell yourself, are rational.

In addition to the questions in Figure 2a, I am providing related questions that I typically use as Rational Mental Filters for the purpose of screening out irrational thoughts and stories. Again, these questions are designed to help you ensure that your stream of thought is aligned with and supportive of your new, rational Life Scripts. They will also help you screen out thoughts that simply do not help feel the way you want to feel and get what you want in life. They include the following:

- Is this belief or thought logical?

- Is it consistent with known facts and reality?

- Will it help me feel the way I want to feel?

- Does it contribute to my rational Life Scripts?

- Will it improve my sense of well-being, happiness, or serenity?

- Will it help me solve my problems?

- Will it help me achieve my goals and live my life in a manner that is consistent with my new Life Scripts?

If you answer no to any of these questions, you must discard the thought and the story connected with the thought. Conversely, if you answer yes to all of the questions, the thought or belief is rational and will support you in your efforts to consistently think and live in a manner that is consistent with your new Life Scripts.

The process of repeatedly monitoring your thoughts, evaluating your thoughts, and discarding those thoughts and stories that you deem to be irrational is the first step to changing maladaptive thoughts to more rational ones. The second step is replacement. Because you simply cannot stop thinking, when you do discard a thought, you must replace it with another thought. This concept is further illustrated in Figure 2b.

Figure 2b
The Thoughts, Emotions, (Re)Actions Diagram
With Space for New Rational Filters and "INSTEAD OFs"

What are the questions you are going to ask yourself to filter out irrational thoughts?

What are you going to think INSTEAD OF the thoughts you put in the trash can?

As you can see in Figure 2b, I have provided you with a place to record the thoughts and stories you plan to think "INSTEAD OF" the thoughts you put in the virtual trashcan. Once again, these INSTEAD OFs must be rational, in that they are logical, consistent with known facts and reality, help you feel the way you want to feel, and align with and support your new Life Scripts.

To help you apply this process in your own life, I have provided you with the following table, which has two columns. Column 1 is where you write down your Rational Mental Filter questions as depicted in Figures 2a and 2b. Column 2 is where you begin to write out the replacement thoughts and stories you will tell yourself INSTEAD OF the irrational thoughts and stories you discard. Because you will need more space than what is provided here, I suggest that you design a similar table that you can use to record your INSTEAD OF thoughts and Life Scripts as you continually strive to replace your irrational thoughts.

Rational Mental Filter Questions	Thoughts I am Going to Think INSTEAD OF the Thoughts I "Put in the Trash"

Hopefully, what has been described and illustrated in this ACT will help you understand that with some advance planning, it's within your power to 1) restructure maladaptive Life Scripts into rational Life Scripts that help you change your life and 2) proactively monitor your thoughts and stories in a way that ensures that you will continue to follow the script that reflects the "new character" represented by what your life goals described in ACT I. Parts 1 and 2 in ACT IV of the LSR

FINAL ACT AND POSTSCRIPT

LIFE SCRIPT RESTRUCTURING "LITE" WITH EXAMPLES

So as not to leave the impression that Life Script Restructuring (LSR) is a difficult process, I want to summarize the process here in a "Lite Version." Once you have gone through the book and understand the principles, you can return to this section as a brief reminder of the process.

The four steps or, as I refer to them here, ACTS, in the process are included here for your ready reference. They include:

ACT I: Decide what you want in your life. Do this by creating a Rational Personal Vision Statement and identifying goals to help you operationalize this vision of what you want to be, know, do, feel, and acquire in your life.

ACT II: Identify irrational thoughts and Life Scripts (using Erikson's eight stages of development) that undermine your ability to live the kind of life you want to live based on your work in ACT I.

ACT III: Restructure (Edit or Re-Write) the irrational Life Scripts you identified in ACT II. Evaluate and continue to revise these scripts until they are rational.

ACT IV: Mentally program and internalize your new, rational Life Scripts using visualization and mental imagery techniques. Use mental monitoring techniques to systematically observe and align your psyche with your new, rational Life Scripts.

That's it. It's so simple, even young children can do it. In fact, even though I do not typically see young children in my practice, when I do occasionally agree to work with a child in using the LSR process, I am always amazed at how quickly he or she picks up on and applies the process. At the time I wrote this book, there were at least two young children with whom I worked who were featured on the Web site www.truepsychology.org. They include seven-year-old Lilly Rose and eight-year-old Liam.

In Lilly's case, she was struggling in school. When I asked her, "Lilly, what story are you telling yourself that is making you upset?" She said, "I have the meanest teacher in the world!" I then explained to her that I help children change the upsetting stories they tell themselves to stories that make them feel happy or calm. Lilly quickly understood and was anxious to try what I called at the time "True Psychology."

Almost immediately, seven-year-old Lilly started using her imagination to change her story. Literally, within 5 minutes she had a new Life Script as it related to her school experience. As you will see if you watch her video at www.truepsychology.org, her new story was a simple one. It was something like "I have a really good teacher this year. She is going to teach me a lot, and I am going to learn a lot!" That was it, and it did the trick. Lilly was OK!

When I watched the camera crew video of Lilly telling her new story, I was blown away. She sat up straight and was insistent that they continue to redo the shot until she got her story "exactly right!"

In a follow-up interview with Lilly I simply asked her, "Hey Lilly, how's school?" Her answer was simply, "I love it!" I then asked, "How is your teacher?" Again, her answer was simple yet profound, "I have a really good teacher. She is teaching me a lot!" She then started telling me all the things she had learned during the past few days.

Liam's "old" story or Life Script was much different than Lilly's. However, the result was the same. When I met with Liam, he told me his story. He had apparently been stuck in an elevator in a mall in Los Angeles. Because of this, he was not willing to ride in elevators. He said, "I am afraid to ride in elevators because I am afraid I will get stuck again." When I told him about the "True Psychology" method, he was skeptical and very hesitant to change his story.

I then said, "Liam, did you know it's a lot safer to ride on an elevator than it is to walk up and down stairs?" He said, "How do you know?" I then pulled out my smartphone and we searched for deaths and injuries from falling down stairs during 2012. Frankly, both he and I were shocked when we realized how many people are either injured or killed on stairs. We then looked up deaths and injuries on elevators during the same time period. We could not find anything. I could tell Liam was ready to change his story so I, once again, explained the process. Just as was the case with Lilly, Liam immediately engaged his imagination and came up with a new story and a plan to practice the story using mental imagery, the "Mental Home Movie Theater" technique described in ACT IV.

When Liam told his story in front of the camera, it was, like Lilly's, very simple. It was something like "I was afraid to ride on an elevator because I didn't want to get stuck again. I made my family walk up and down lots of stairs." He then said, "Then I used True Psychology to change my story. I closed my eyes and watched myself going up and down on an elevator without getting stuck. I'm not afraid to ride on an elevator anymore!

In a follow-up interview a month after Liam's interview in front of the cameras, I asked him, "Hey Liam, are you OK with riding on elevators?" He said, "Yes, of course!" Wow!

You will see others on the Web site who will tell similar stories of seeming miraculous changes that resulted from changing their Life Scripts. Frankly, the miraculous nature of these changes is not all that difficult to understand; our minds are neutral about the information we put in them and the thoughts and stories we "decide" to entertain or scare ourselves with. It's similar to what I experience when I plant my garden. If I plant cucumber seeds, I get cucumbers. If I plant carrots, I get carrots. If I plant corn, I get corn! Similarly, if you plant and entertain calm, encouraging thoughts, you will become calm and encouraged. If you plant frightening thoughts, you will become scared and even paranoid. I witnessed one of the best examples of this Garbage In/Garbage Out (GI/GO) concept when interviewing one of my teenage clients.

This young woman, who was at the time a junior in high school, said her parents wanted me to help her understand why she was so paranoid. After she explained her symptoms (which included a feeling when she gets up at night that someone is behind her and is trying to "sneak up on me and hurt me"), I started asking her a number of questions. Given her age, I started with trying to understand the type of media she consumed. When she started talking about her television and movie preferences, I knew I had the answer to her parents' question. She said, "I love to watch crime, gangster and horror movies. In fact, I watch a horror movie almost every night before I go to bed." After hearing this I said, "Well then, I diagnose you as being perfectly normal. Because of the type of information you put in your mind and because you do it almost every night before bed, of course you will experience fear and paranoia during the night. If you want to overcome this fear you will need to change your television and movie viewing preferences to include the type of programming that helps you think the kind of thoughts that help you feel the way you want to feel, which is 'not afraid and paranoid.'" She was satisfied with my diagnosis, as were her parents.

Frankly, I don't know if she made changes because as she left the office she said, "I think I am going to be OK," and she never came back. I do know, however, that the GI/GO principle works with all of us. If you put garbage in your mind, your thoughts and behaviors will reflect the type of information you take in. This is why pornography, especially the intense doses that are now available on the Internet, is so debilitating and often causes degenerate behaviors in individuals who were raised in healthy, morally uplifting environments.

On the day before I sent this manuscript to my publisher, a young 12-year-old boy met with me in my office for the first time. He was very upset and crying. When I asked what was going on, he explained that he was preoccupied with the thought of dying. I asked him what caused this feeling and he said, "I saw a horror movie last summer. It was about a family that moved to a new house and a demon tried to get inside the children's heads. He had killed every family who had lived there. This made me think that God wasn't with me and I was going to die and not go to Heaven."

After hearing his story, I told the young man about Life Script Restructuring, and he agreed to work together with me to change his upsetting story. He went from crying to using his imagination, and within minutes we created a new, rational story. His new story is "The truth is, I am a good person. I love God. He knows I love him. I'm not perfect, but I am trying to be like him. My favorite song is 'Lord I Need You'! He loves me and he wants me to be happy and do his work. I will not die until I have done the work I was sent to earth to do. I know that God will guide me to Heaven."

After he finished his new story, I noticed that his demeanor changed completely from appearing to be very anxious and emotional, to very calm and relaxed. When I asked him how he was feeling he said, "I feel calm and safe! I am not as worried as I was before. I feel good!" I then gave the young man an assignment to watch and listen to videos that support his new story, just before bed each night. Although I will follow up in a week, based on previous experiences I am certain that this young man is going to be OK.

Finally, the "secret weapon" of Life Script Restructuring is how the technique leverages brain plasticity to bring about permanent change. According to relatively recent neurological research, our brains have the ability to rewire themselves in response to changes in our thinking (neuroplasticity). This is why I believe that by implementing LSR, you do have the ability to permanently change irrational Life Scripts and permanently replace them with rational scripts that will continually dictate rational thoughts and actions.

As I mentioned at the beginning, LSR works because it's grounded in my clinical experience and based on what leading behavioral scientists agree are the key universal principles required to help individuals make permanent changes and reach their potential.

Obviously, I believe in LSR and strongly recommend that you begin the process of rewriting the parts of your Life Script(s) that are not currently working for you. As the star of your own "movie," you can rewrite scripts to achieve a happy ending.

No man can run away from weakness. He must either fight it out or perish. And if that be so . . . why not now, and where you stand. - Robert Louis Stevenson

ABOUT THE AUTHOR

Dr. Galen Cole, PhD, MPH, DAPA, LPC, is a licensed counselor and board certified psychotherapist. His certifications include: National Certified Counselor (NCC), National Board of Certified Counselors; Board Certified Professional Counselor (BCPC) and Diplomat (DAPA), American Psychotherapy Association; Certified Relationship Specialist (CRS), American Psychotherapy Association; Cognitive Behavioral Therapy (CBT), National Association of Cognitive Behavioral Therapists; and Equine Assisted Psychotherapy (EAP), Equine Assisted Growth and Learning Association.

As a therapist, he provides individual, couple, and family counseling. He has extensive training and experience in clinical counseling psychology, psychotherapy, psychiatric epidemiology, behavioral science research, education, mass and interpersonal communication, and public health. He has taught counseling psychology, equine assisted mental health, behavioral and evaluation research, and a number of other counseling and health-related courses at the university level.

He has been on the undergraduate and/or graduate faculty at Northern Arizona University, Arizona State University,

Pennsylvania State University, and Emory University. Dr. Cole has extensive experience practicing what he teaches, including working on staff and as a consultant at numerous clinics, hospitals, and community based organizations; consulting on a number of popular television series; serving as the executive director of a 501c3 foundation; working as an assistant director of the county public health department in Phoenix, Arizona; and working for 22 years as a behavioral scientist and director of research, evaluation, and communication activities in various centers, institutes, and offices at the U.S. Centers for Disease Control and Prevention (CDC) in Atlanta, Georgia.

In 2003, Dr. Cole was appointed by the Governor of Georgia to serve on the Georgia Human Resources (DHR) Board. In this capacity he served as chair of the DHR committee that provided policy guidance to the state Division of Mental Health, Developmental Disabilities, and Addictive Diseases. He has served on the American Psychotherapy Association's Board of Professional Counselors. He currently serves as the Ethics Chair on the Board of the Georgia Association of Licensed Professional Counselors. Dr. Cole has been a trainer and consultant in the Central Asian Republics, Nigeria, China, Thailand, Kenya, Switzerland, Australia, Peru, Germany, Uganda, and the Middle East, where he has consulted and conducted trainings with the Palestinian Health Authority, the Israeli Ministry of Health, and many other NGOs.

He has also provided technical support to a number of prominent international organizations, including the United Nations Children's Fund (UNICEF); the Pan American Health Organization (PAHO); the World Bank; Hollywood, Health and

Society (HH&S); and the World Health Organization (WHO). Dr. Cole has published numerous books and scientific papers and made presentations at conferences and training seminars across the world. In recognition of his many accomplishments, Dr. Cole has received distinguished alumni awards from two of the universities he attended. Dr. Cole and his wife, Priscilla, have been married for 38 years and are the parents of 5 adult children.

References

COLE, G.E. (2013) True Psychology: A Scientific Approach to a Better Life. Aphalon Firth Publishers, Atlanta, GA.

DEINER, E. (2000). Subjective well-being: The science of happiness and a proposal for a national index. American Psychologist, Vol 55(1), pp. 34-43.

ELLIS, A., HARPER, R. A. & POWERS, M. (1975). A New Guide to Rational Living. Wilshire Book Company.

ERIKSON, E. H. (1963). Childhood and Society. 2nd Ed. New York: W.W. Norton and C. ERIKSON, E. H. (1968). Identity: Youth and Crisis. New York: Norton.

GREENBERG, B., SALMON, C., PATEL, D., BECK, V. & COLE, G. E. (2004). Evolution of an Entertainment Education Research Agenda in Cody, M.J., Singhal, A., Sabido, M., & Rogers, E.M. (Eds.) Entertainment-Education Worldwide: History, Research, and Practice. Mahaw, NJ: Lawrence Erlbaum Associates, Publishers.

HANSON, R. & MENDIUS, R. (2009) Buddha's Brain: The Practical Neuroscience of Happiness, Love, and Wisdom. Oakland, CA: New Harbinger Publication.

KOHLBERG, L. (1969), Stage and Sequence, Handbook of Socialization Theory and Research, McGraw Hill: New York. LEWIN, K. (1952). Field Theory in Social Science: Selected Theoretical Papers by Kurt Lewin. London: Tavistock.

MARCIA, JAMES E. (1966). Development and Validation of Ego Identity Status. Journal of Personality and Social Psychology 3: 551–558. 2012-01-28.

MCADAMS, D. P. (2001). The Psychology of Life Stories.
Review of general psychology, 5(2), 100. PIAGET, J. (1972).
The Psychology of the Child. New York: Basic Books.

ROSENTHAL, E.L., DE CASTRO BUFFINGTON,
S. & COLE, G.E. (2013). Covering Cancer:
Examining the Incidence and Impact of Prime Time
Television Cancer Storylines. Presentation at the
National Conference on Health Communication,
Marketing and Media. Atlanta, GA: August, 2013.

SELIGMAN, M. E. P. (2012). Flourish: A Visionary
New Understanding of Happiness and Well-being.

SOKOL, J. T. (2009) Identity Development Throughout the
Lifetime: An Examination of Eriksonian Theory, Graduate
Journal of Counseling Psychology: Vol. 1: Iss. 2, Article 14.

VYGOTSKY, L. S. (1978). Mind in Society: The
Development of Higher Psychological Proceses. Chapter
6 Interaction between learning and development (79-
91). Cambridge, MA: Harvard University Press.

WALLIS, C. (2005). "Science of Happiness: New
Research on Mood, Satisfaction". TIME.

Made in the USA
San Bernardino, CA
04 September 2017